Keep On Working

Books by Jim Christy

The New Refugees: American Voices in Canada, editor
    (Peter Martin Associates, 1972)
Beyond the Spectacle, essays
Palatine Cat, poems (Four Humours Press, 1978)
Rough Road to the North, travel
Streethearts, novel
Traveling Light, stories
The Price of Power
Flesh and Blood
Letter from the Khyber Pass, CD and intro
Strange Sites: Uncommon Homes & Gardens of the Pacific Northwest
    with photographs by Alex Waterhouse-Hayward
    & Lionel Trudel & Felix Keskula
The Sunnyside of the Deathhouse
The BUK Book, Musings on Charles Bukowski
    with photos by Claude Powell
Shanghai Alley, novel (Ekstasis, 1997)
The Long Slow Death of Jack Kerouac
Junkman, stories
Between the Meridians, travel stories
Princess and Gore
Terminal Avenue
Tight Like That
The Redemption of Anna Dupree
Scalawags: Rogues, Roustabouts, Wags & Scamps
Nine O'Clock Gun
Marimba Forever
Sweet Assorted: 118 Takes From a Tin Box
Real Gone
The Cockeyed World
The Big Thirst and other Doggone Poems
Rogues, Rascals, and Scalawags Too: Ne'er-Do-Wells Through the Ages
Rough Road to the North: A Vagabond on the Great Northern Highway
The Cockeyed World
Real Gone

Keep On Working

Jim Christy

Ekstasis Editions

Copyright © Jim Christy 2025
Cover art: Jim Christy

Published in 2025 by:
Ekstasis Editions Canada Ltd.
Box 8474, Main Postal Outlet
Victoria, B.C. V8W 3S1

All rights reserved. No part of this book may be reproduced in any form without the written permission of the publisher, with the exception of brief passages in reviews. Any request for photocopying or other reproduction of any part of this book should be directed in writing to the publisher or to ACCESS: The Canadian Copyright Licensing Agency, One Yonge Street, Suite 800, Toronto, Ontario, Canada, M5E 1E5.

LIBRARY AND ARCHIVES CANADA CATALOGUING IN PUBLICATION

TITLE: Keep on working / Jim Christy.
NAMES: Christy, Jim, 1945- author
IDENTIFIERS: Canadiana 20250107058 | ISBN 9781771715874 (hardcover) | ISBN 9781771715867 (softcover)
SUBJECTS: LCGFT: Memoir.
CLASSIFICATION: LCC PS8555.H74 K44 2025 | DDC C814/.54—DC23

Printed and bound in Canada.

Keep On Working

Just the other day, I found myself wishing I had a job. Almost immedately, I considered slapping myself upside the head to dispel such an absurd notion. But what the hell, I'm ready to try something new, even a job. But, hopefully, one unlike all the dumb jobs in my past.

The trouble is I'm near the end of my Seventies with a panoply of health problems so I won't be lifting that bale and toting that barge. Also, I no longer even have a driver's license. Me applying for a job or calling at an employment agency has the makings of a comedy sketch. I can imagine the look on the interviewer's face when he or she reads the numbers I've written in the space for 'date of birth.'

Yes, ma'am I'm willing to accept an entry level position and hopefully work my way up the ladder. Of course, I'm capable of lifting that coffee pot. I see you have a good retirement plan; fine, I figure I'll be well set up when I retire at one hundred and twenty-one.

There'd been times in my life that I've abhorred the very idea of working for someone else. But for a person who's long thought that way I've spent a lot of time actually doing it. I started early and as a little kid and loved the idea of having my own money.

I was self-employed then, a real little hustling entrepreneur. It's difficult to imagine myself doing all that.

Later, I figured work was an impediment to what I considered as my freedom. But it enabled me to go on trips. Work a couple of months and take off for Paris or Caracas. When I wasn't saving for a trip, I was buying time to write, working dumb jobs in order to hole up in a Toronto rooming house to type away long into the night.

I had a friend in Toronto, my only writer friend. He was a sucessful freelancer mainly because he would write about anything and adjust his opinions according to the editorial requirements of the magazine or newspaper that gave him the assignment. I was choosier but yet for a few years in the Seventies was able to make some decent part time money at writing. There were actually magazines wanting articles, and they were willing to pay well for them.

But on more than one afternoon when I was raking wet leaves or digging post holes in the rain, I cursed my so-called 'purity' and thought of my friend cozy and warm in his apartment, seated before his Royal Standard, mug of coffee at hand, composing an article.

I worked for some nasty human beings, some of whom I grew to despise but I also worked alongside some great people. There's a camaraderie that develops when you're working well beside another man, especially if troubles arise and you have to work through them Of course, I found this only on manual labour jobs; maybe it develops between white collar workers, too, I don't know.

There's nothing ennobling about work. Wielding a hammer or a pitchfork I never pictured myself as some heroic figure on a Russian social realist poster.

Some of the work was pleasant enough, some of it might even be considered fun but too much of it was drudgery—boring and ill-paid, like operating a drill press or a stamping machine. Other work that some considered demeaning or insulting to their being I did without qualm. I cleaned out stables in Pennsylvania horse country. So, you were shifting around pitchforks of hay and shoveling horse manure, big deal. Digging ditches was no fun but you were outside and talking to the guy on the next shovel. Digging post holes was awkward and hard work. I didn't mind my brief stint at grave digging at a Vancouver cemetery; most of it was done with a bobcat, the shovel work consisting mainly of shaping and trimming the edges.

A friend of mine recently commented that I was 'job hopping' and I was at one time a 'curb hopper' which was what they called the employee who took orders from, and delivered them to, cars parked at the curb outside a restaurant.

A few times in Toronto I went out picking worms. You'd meet up at one of the golf courses early in the morning with a large empty juice can strapped to your lower leg. You were handed a light and, bent over, set about picking large earth worms from the dewy ground.

Also, during this same time, there was work at construction sites where walls or entire buildings had been torn down. There would be mounds of bricks scattered around. You picked your mound and with a claw hammer had to ship the old mortar off the brick. You were paid piece work. None of this bothered me although I would rather have not been doing it. I wasn't doing it for 'experience' or for raw material to write about as a couple of fools did who I was aware of.

I certainly never felt sorry for myself. The ones I had sympathy for were those that went at it every day at set hours. That was my idea of hell. I asked myself why they did it, how could they do it?

I would think of men and women with families going to their jobs, chained to the endless process. They were heroic in their way, meeting their responsibilities like that. Riding the subway, switching to the bus, barely making it in on time in order to satisfy the clock.

It's the ones who don't have to do it, for whom I had little sympathy. Some of them were just dullards lacking in imagination, others kept going solely because of the lure of 'stuff,' consumer goods. Therein lies the strength of capitalism. People don't need to be chained to the job or enslaved by ideology. They don't labour under the belief they're keeping their country strong. No, it's work, work. work, and you can get that boat. That car. Won't they look 'cool' parked in the driveway of your home where you live with the wife and two kids although the house is big enough for twenty Cambodians.

And don't forget the computers and the sixty-inch tv, and the gadgets that will need updating next year or next week. And the kids need three hundred dollar runners or the other kids will make fun of them.

There's no end of it except the end of you.

But you say you want a revolution? Fat chance,

Don't make me laugh.

Historically, at least in the twentieth century, revolutions have been brought about by intellectuals and workers.

These days the former are moribund and the latter want those same boats and satellite phones so they can always have the porn sites at hand. They're a long way from Wobblies.

I dreamed I saw Joe Hill last night. Alive as you and me, and spinning in his grave.

I was washing dishes next to the black kid in the kitchen of a Spanish Restaurant in Saint Augustine, Florida in 1976; I was thirty-one years old and Ned was eighteen. I had been enlisted to help out Sherry the owner who was the new girl friend of my buddy Marcel Horne. The regular dishwasher, a white guy, had quit at the prospect of having to work next to a black person, although he didn't refer to the kid as a black person or a negro. Ned was nervous about me being there beside him. I figured out right away why this was so. I told him not to worry about it. After a couple of nights, he felt comfortable enough to tell me he'd never been so close to a white person before. "Well, I'm Canadian," I said, skipping over my Virginia birth and Philadelphia up-bringing. "It's different up there."

"You mean black and whites work together?"

He regarded this as a kind of revelation.

"Not only that but they live in the same neighbourhoods and often in the same houses. And nobody bothers anybody else." which was basically true.

Marcel Horne was my best friend. I knew St. Augustine, and he came down from Toronto for the winter. He thought he might try his luck in the ancient city because he wasn't having any in Toronto. Marcel was a fire breather, not a fire eater; either way employment wasn't easy to find in that particular line of endeavour.

There was a fellow in town named Al Tesori whom I bought a car from every winter that I spent in St. Augustine. Not long before Marcel showed up, Al sold me a beautiful tan Buick Electra 225. The plan was for me to accompany my pal to look for work in the clubs up and down the Florida coast. We did that, too but didn't find any work. Marcel would hang back while I talked to the owner about what a unique act it was. I mentioned that Marcel could do a simple fire breathing set or an extended one with music and a light show. (I did the light show part.) The club owners always wanted a full show audition with no pay. I told them this was too demanding to do for free. Marcel risked his life every time he did a performance. The reason Marcel hung back was not only because he was shy but he was also physically intimidating, six foot four, two hundred forty pounds, beefy sloping shoulders and huge arms with a gargoyle face tattooed on each bicep. He looked like he went down to the clubhouse whenever he was bored and beat up a couple of Hell's Angels for something to do. But he was one of the gentlest men I would ever meet.

I knew him for ten years until his death and all that time we only went into a bar together one time. He avoided bars, taverns and pubs because there was inevitably someone who wanted to test him

Sherry was a friend of a friend of mine, I introduced her to Marcel and they hit it off. Marcel moved in to a trailer out back of the restaurant. Sherry's husband was Spanish, he had started the restaurant and supervised the cooking but he ran out, leaving her with the business. She had no experience at such a thing and no notion of Spanish cuisine. But she had rent to pay. Sherry bought a Spanish cookbook and hired Marcel to be the unlikely waiter. I told him he should just glare at people and demand they order the most expensive thing on the menu– or else.

One busy night, Sherry wanted to send me out on the floor to wait tables but Marcel dissuaded her of the notion. He put up with rude behaviour which I wouldn't have stood for. That's how I became a dishwasher.

One night Ned apologized because he would have liked to have me come to dinner at his house. He had told his mother about his white friend, and she wanted to meet me. "But I can't invite you," he said.
I asked him why but I had an idea why, and I was right.

"It's my father. He hates white people."

That, of course, was not difficult to understand.

So, we restricted our socializing to talking and laughing over our adjoining sinks. We couldn't even get a coffee or a beer together at the Spanish Armada, the tavern next door. They wouldn't have served us. No one down there paid any attention to any civil rights bill.

As a kid, I was always interested in what the grown ups around me did for a living. My father was what was known as a ward heeler. The Democratic Party controlled Philadelphia, and the Mob exerted more than a little influence on the Democratic Party. I would go around the streets with the old man who paid calls at flower shops or the back rooms of Italian social clubs. Suffice it to say there was a heavy Italian influence in all this. He was born a week after the boat from Italy landed in Philadelphia. His father was later given a job as a ditch digger, his reward for working for the Party. During Prohibition, my grandfather operated a still in his basement and my father spent his youth delivering bootleg liquor. After the War my father got a job with the police fingerprint department and began his political career. A few years later he got into the 'insurance' business. For two or three years, he had a small office at the back of a Buick dealership where a certain criminal element bought their cars. Members of the Mob drove Buicks and Oldsmobiles not Cadillacs.

He had three first cousins, brothers Pat, Ange and Sonny Boy. For decades the first two owned and operated Pat's Taproom on Passyunk Avenue in South Philadelphia. I spent a lot of time in their as a kid, hanging out in the backroom where there was a battered old upright piano or in the front room sitting in the sawdust under the dartboard. And there I was one Saturday morning making roads in the sawdust with my hand when a loud voice behind me called "Lamby!"

This was a sharply dressed Jewish man with slicked back hair who wore double breasted suits. He was the only non-Italian guy in the 'gang.'

Lamby spun around on his stool to face the voice. I looked and saw a man holding a gun that he pointed at Lamby who shouted, "No!" as the bullets ripped into him.

I don't have a clear memory of what happened next but there was a struggle between several men and they all hustled out through the swing doors.

Sonny Boy was the mysterious brother. I didn't see him as much as the others. He was a husky man with oily black hair, always shouting or laughing. He drove a delivery truck for the *Daily News*. I remember his hands all ink-stained, the bundle wires had made permanent creases in his palms. Whatever happened to him I don't know. As for Pat, he and Adele divorced and I met him years later when I was in my early twenties and went back to south Philadelphia for awhile. I rented a room on Mifflin Street and discovered he was my neighbour and living in his own room. Quite a change from the apartment over the taproom where he had lived with Adele and their sons Robby and Tommy. You could step out the kitchen door onto a roof like a big room with tables and awnings. It was a great place for weekend afternoon parties where all sorts of characters show up, cops, criminals, boxers, old country moustachios and a dozen kids.

Ange was my favourite uncle. He had a deep, rumbling voice and looked like the black jazz singer Isaac Prysock. Ange made the best pasta sauce I've ever tasted. He'd put a small pork roast in a deep pan in the morning, cover it with canned tomatoes and tomato paste and let it simmer until dinner time.

After Pat separated from Adele and moved away, Ange ran the bar himself. Over the years and decades, the clientele changed as the neighbourhood changed, from Italian and Jewish to black. By the early Eighties it was all black, the whites having moved away, mostly to the white suburbs of South Jersey.

One afternoon when Ange was tending bar, another man pointing a handgun came in shouting, "This is a hold up!' The patrons held up their hands and the gunman, a black man named Greene, announced, "You black people don't have anything to worry about." And then he shot and killed my uncle Ange.

My father's sister Lena was married to Joe Verichio and they had a luncheonette at Fifth and Catherine Streets.

His other sister Sylvia was married to a tall man named Tony who was a janitor at a school somewhere. As a little kid I recall him in the living room of the narrow house where we lived on Reese Street. He raised his arms like he was going to fly and was able to touch the walls on either side of the room.

There were men on my mother's side of the family, men of the late nineteenth century, who were no strangers to guns. These were the Clantons, the brothers murdered by Earps and their syphilitic junkie dentist friend Doc Holiday in Tombstone, Arizona.

The first time the word 'cowboy' was ever used it was to describe the Clantons and their friends the McLaury brothers. Their trade was cattle rustling. Outlaws sure but worse than that, for them, was the fact that they were political opponents of the Earps. Despite a hundred movies about the notorious incident in 1881, the Clantons and McLaurys were unarmed when the Earps opened fire.

My grandmother was born a month or so before the shootings. I like to imagine that Ike or Billy had heard the news and were thinking about their brand new niece when the Earps opened fire.

My maternal grandfather, Clarence Runyon Dolby had been an itinerate carpenter, following in the footsteps of his father. Following literally because they drifted south from rural Pennsylvania, plying their trade along the way until they reached southern Virginia.

When I was a boy hanging around him, my grandfather tended a few acres of corn and beans. He also had grapevines and apple trees. He had a rural mail route, too and often I'd go out with him on his route sticking mail in the boxes and taking it out, saving him the need to reach over and roll down the window to do it.

He and his father built the huge house where my grand parents lived and where my mother and her sister and brother were born and raised.

He could make anything. He built the barn and the out buildings. I was proud of the tomahawk he fashioned for me, I remember it with a red and white blade, everything heavily varnished. My grandmother didn't care for the tomahawk, her being half Rappahannock.

As well as being interested in jobs that other people did, I loved the calls and cries of hawkers. I consider myself fortunate to have reached consciousness before the mass media take over of north America, before the great leveller of franchise restaurants and interchangeable shopping malls. Instead of neighbourhood merchants you suddenly had the same stores with the same signs and the same goods for sale, the same radio commercials touting the same stuff.

When I was growing up in Philadelphia, produce wagons pulled by horses still came around, and the driver or his assistant, often a kid, often a kid, no older than me, would holler "Carrots. Cabbage, I got fresh spinach". Meanwhile, the bridle rattled at regular intervals the driver snapped the reins and the sound of the leather on the horses back made a counterpoint to the clopping hoofs.

And there were the hawkers pushing or pulling their carts announcing their approach. Each one had his chant which often turned to song. I recall the knife grinder, the candy man and most especially the man selling those delicious soft pretzels. His cart looked like a mini coach, the thick pretzels waiting behind the glass. At the front was a wooden rack that held jars of mustard, sauerkraut and even ketchup, for those foolish enough to ruin a pretzel with the stuff. In each jar was a wooden fork-like object for spreading the contents. I used to think of this fork being used all day everyday. Pretzel's come get your soft hot pretzels. You know you want 'em so don't delay. So good they won't last all day.

I had no way of knowing that these itinerant merchants were everywhere in the world and they all had their chants and pitches. In the 1800s in London the merchants and the cries themselves became famous, so much so that they started showing up on the tobacco tins and tea towels.

There was a famous hawker in London in Georgian times known as Tiddy Doll who baked and sold gingerbread men. He wore white silk stockings, gold buckled shoes and sported an ostrich plume in his hat. His cries were quoted all over town and he shows up in several memoirs of the time.

But there were innumerable itinerant merchants and repairmen wandering Europe and the world, cobblers, tinkerers, hurdy gurdy men with monkeys. Up until the early Seventies there was a organ grinder and his monkey out front of the CP Rail station in Vancouver.

I learned that many of these hawkers were ambitious tramps who wandered specific areas with their trade goods. Others covered great distances and purchased goods closer to their destinations. I was fascinated by these people and by tramps themselves.

It should be emphasized that tramps were not bums. They walked and would work if it was necessary whereas hobos rode freights and actively sought work. A bum neither worked nor walked nor rode; he mainly just drank.

Later vagabonding about the country I met many legitimate tramps (as opposed to hikers). Somewhere in Maryland I encountered a skinny old man with a long thin white beard who tramped from Maine to Florida and back every year. He had a supply of pocket-sized notebooks wherein he jotted down his poems and observations.

In general, these people were looked down upon, at least they were in the United States. There is and was no tolerance for tramps in America regardless of bogus claims of freedom. In other countries like Russia there is a long tradition of tramping, of wandering scholars and holy men. in New Zealand and Australia the anthem of the People, "Waltzing Matilda" is a tramp poem turned into song.

Tramps and hobos, and the very idea of them, seemed to offend something in the America psyche, as did carnival and circus folk. Americans couldn't explain what it was except it's 'not right'. A tramp often risked his life by simply walking down a road in the U. S. of A., a target of cops, of beer and pop cans thrown by teenagers in cars and worse from adults. The latter might let off a gun shot or two. That happened to me on a side road in southwestern Pennsylvania.

In the carnivals I was ashamed and embarrassed at the way the freaks were jeered and hollered at. Away from the sideshow conditions were horrible for them. Out of this crisis was born Gibtown, near Tampa, Florida. It was sort of a protected village where carnies retreated when the season closed in in the winter. They could move about freely without being harassed and stared at.

But it wasn't always like that. At least in certain areas. It seemed to be all right if freaks were on stage or behind glass or were the objects of lectures.

For years there was an establishment on Scollay Square in Boston, called Austin and Stone's Museum where for a couple of decades, a man known as Professor Hutchings held court. He kept audiences in thrall with his speeches on freaks. Hutchings had been a child math prodigy and once worked in P. T. Barnum's Museum where he was billed as 'the Lightning Calculator.'

Often his lecture would include a living example. Professor Hutchings gave his first in 1883 and continued until he passed away in 1911. It is calculated that he did 30,00 of these lectures.

There were numerous legendary tramps throughout the world, though you had to be at least somewhat familiar with that world to know of them, people like Josiah Flynt, Stephan Graham, Long Legged Jack from the Isthmus, Cy Slade, Kathleen Phelan, and my very favourite, a hero of mine, in fact, a Kiwi called Barney White Rats who travelled around New Zealand giving shows for children. He was what is known there as a swagger

He walked the country for decades, having arrived by ship from London where he was a circus performer. Somewhere on some north Island road, he came up with the idea of doing shows with trained white mice that came to be called rats and a magic lantern. He was immensely popular in the schools and kids nearly rioted with anticipation when they learned he was about to show up at theirs.

There is the legend of a tramp kingdom in Scotland and another about Tafur, the King of the tramps, a Norman knight who threw down his arms and set out on the road. Soon he had given up his clothes as well and walked naked at the head of processions of followers of Peter the Hermit. He carried no provisions, eating only what he could gather along the way.

I was pulling up tent pegs one afternoon in with the alligator man in Indiana when the townies showed up wielding crowbars and baseball bats. There were a couple of guards hired to keep the locals off the lot but they must have been playing cards or dozing off under a truck or probably they just looked the other way.

I had picked up a copy of *Amusement Business*, the bible of show people, at a newsstand in Akron Ohio, and came across a notice indicating a roughie was needed, immediately, with Shaw-Daks Shows. The outfit's itinerary for the week was given and I figured I'd be able to catch them at the tear down in Kokomo, Indiana.

I set off right away but got nabbed almost immediately, in Canton, Ohio, for hitchhiking on the interstate. I had just gotten a ride down the Akron-Canton Corridor, as they called it, and it was a peculiar ride, indeed. Looking back, the whole experience is, well, if not exactly funny, certainly ridiculous.

So they had nearly finished the tear down by the time I reached Kokomo. I helped with the tents and loaded gear and rode in the back of a truck during the run south to French Lick.

The set-up went well and the next evening I was on the bally assisting the talker in drawing a tip. It wasn't what I was hired for but the talker seemed to think I could turn a phrase so he had me stand to the side and toss in comments now and again. There was a half-and-half and a fire-eater/sword swallower; a fat woman and the alligator boy. His name was Leland Stovall and he was by far the most popular attraction on the lot, save for the girl show.

The thing that made Leland popular, as well as drawing the ire of some of the rednecks, was that he looked like he was one of them except for what was a virulent case of ichthyosis vulgaris. He skin was dry and scaly with large light brown scales that resembled nothing so much as flakes of breakfast cereal. He would appear in just his slacks and the yokels would stare open mouthed at his upper body. Leland always gave a little shake before disappearing behind the curtain, leaving a puddle of scales where he stood.

Later when I saw him taking a shower around back of the mess tent, I learned that the condition had not spared an inch of him. Standing there under the shower contraption, he resembled a large white and brown spotted fish standing on its tail fin.

He was a nice fellow, careful about his appearance. He trimmed his fingernails and his toenails, used Vitalis on his hair, parted it on one side and kept it cut short. When he wasn't performing, Leland could usually be found sitting in the shade of a truck or tent reading western novels or rubbing moisturizing lotion on his skin. He was very polite, too. If he went visiting he always swept up any scales he'd left behind.

He liked to talk about his western novels and about western movies which he called 'oaters' or 'dusters'. I hadn't read very many westerns although I did give Ernest Haycox a try, mainly because Kenneth Rexroth, a poet and essayist whom I admired, had written that Haycox was a far more important writer than William Faulkner. A ludicrous statement but I came to suspect that Rexroth liked to see what he could get away with.

But I could hold my own with the Alligator Man when it came to oaters. He would try me with questions, like, "I guess you know who shot Liberty Vallance, don't you?"

"Sure," I answered. "Did you know William S. Hart was a real cowboy?"

On and on it went.

So, we were working side by side, pulling up tent pegs after the run in Dubuque when the townies attacked and the "Hey Rube!" rang out. No one knew exactly what caused the fracas, not that Townies ever needed a reason. They hated the sideshow freaks and the operators, figuring none of either category could be decent people like they were. Maybe one of them developed funny feelings about Bobby/Bobbi the half-and-half or had a mild case of psoriasis and feared winding up like Leland the Alligator Man. Whatever the cause, they came with a vengeance wielding baseball bats and tire irons, some of them carrying American flags.

Some of the carnies engaged directly in the battle, others saw to getting the freaks into trailers and trucks because they were the operation's most valuable assets. The yokels no doubt told themselves they'd be striking a blow for America if they put the boots to a pinhead. Only Jenny the fat lady got into any hand-to-hand combat but the dwarf, Big Marty, used his cut-down bow and arrow from a perch on the roof of a Mack cab and protected by the rise of the trailer. The arrows were metal-tipped and effective.

It was quite a melee, bodies falling and rising all over the lot. The police showed up and hung about the edge of the lot doing little except to rescue a townie whenever one of them seemed to be getting the worst of it along the fringes.

The fighting was fierce; it seemed like it went on for an hour but probably only lasted twenty minutes and might have gone on longer except that someone set fire to the only tent that remained standing. The police jumped in to cordon off the area until the fire trucks showed up.

Not that they were protective of carnival property; no, there were trucks near the tent and a small shopping centre adjacent to the lots.

Leland and I replayed the 'Hey, Rube' long after midnight, drinking cheap package store brandy around the fold-down table in his

17-foot trailer as we rolled west through the dark, Marshall One-Eye, the electrician, driving. I had a cut under my right eye and a fat lip but Leland had escaped injury, at least, injury to his body. If the insults bothered him, he didn't let on. Perhaps he was used to it; God knows he'd heard enough of them. Me, however, I was shocked at what people said to him, and to the other freaks.

That night we had our most intimate conversation. I didn't have much to reveal but Leland did. He told me horrible stories about growing up, his father and mother happily sending him off at the age of fourteen to the carnival after a sideshow operator gave them a sort of signing bonus. How he had a twin brother who was normal and lived in New York City.

Leland sent him money every month. "Not that he needs it because he has a good job and supports a wife and a child quite comfortably. I also send some to my mother and father who are getting on in years. I don't have much else to do with my money."

I stayed with the show for another couple of weeks before abandoning it outside of Denver. I was going to hang around in Denver for a few days before hopping a freight to San Francisco. I wanted to get a ship to Hawaii. After that, I'd probably head back to New York City.

I did.

Rather than having a wife and kid and respectable job in a well-off neighbourhood, Leland's brother was a nasty piece of work, a scabrous junkie who shared a room on Avenue C with several other mean, scabrous junkies. His goal in life was to open his own meth lab. Meanwhile, he broke into cars, climbed up fire escape ladders and got into apartments, and turned tricks to get what he needed to score. He called his brother a freak and an embarrassment. "My brother is the fucking Alligator Man in the fucking circus, man," he announced to the others lying around on piss-stained mattresses.

"Right?" he asked me, to validate his claim.

"It's the carnival, not the circus," I told him.

As I was leaving, he said he'd blow me for fifteen bucks.

I heard them all laughing as I left.

I told Ned about the underground railroad. He had heard of it but thought it was an actual railroad with locomotives belching smoke and kindly white conductors swinging lanterns and risking everything to help escaped slaves on the run. He couldn't believe that all you had to do to be free was to step over the border into Canada. I told him that

I was a draft dodger and had taken that step across the border. I didn't explain that I was working illegally in St. Augustine.

Our stint at the restaurant lasted two months or until the husband came back, promising to mend his ways and do the cooking. By then it was Spring and I went back to Toronto. Marcel who'd thought he had it made took off for Tampa where he hooked up with a carnival, his natural habitat.

Not too long afterwards, he too returned to Toronto and by then I was working for an old employer, David Duplain who had a business he called Geneva Gardens. A few years earlier, I'd answered an ad in the *Toronto Star*, advertising a ten-year-old, yellow Ford pickup truck for sale. When I reached the address on Lonsdale Avenue, I thought I'd seen the seller, David Duplain somewhere before. "I think I know you from somewhere," he said. It turns out we had met in Amsterdam where we stayed at the same hostel. One day we had arranged to meet for dinner. When he didn't show up the fellow at the desk told handed me a note. It was from David who apologized, explaining that he'd met a girl and she was something special. He said that he was sure I'd understand. I didn't have any other contact with David until I answered the ad for the pickup. He explained that the date back in Amsterdam went so well he wound up marrying the girl and bringing her to Canada. Ria was from Geneva and David called his new company Geneva Gardens.

I told him not only was our meeting serendipitous, it was ironic as well because I wanted the truck in order to start my own landscaping business. I didn't buy the pickup but David hired me to work for him which I did for parts of five years.

I liked the work. It was different every day. Sure, I mowed plenty of lawns, used a weed eater, trimmed, planted and pruned, shoveled and raked. There was sod laying and posthole digging. The usual chores of a landscape gardener but David expanded his operations to include construction work. We built fences and patios. I liked the work, learned plenty and became quite versatile; it was also a good way to stay in shape. You went through a range of motions, bending, reaching, lifting, turning, pushing and pulling.

I wasn't new to this kind of thing. My parents moved to the suburbs when I was twelve years old and suddenly there was a little lawn to mow, leaves to rake and azalea bushes to water. There's a part in one of Charles Bukowski's books where he is made to cut the lawn, after which his father gets down on all fours to check for errant leaves of grass, ones that had escaped the blades of the mower. My mother used to do that and if she found even a blade, let alone a patch of errant grass, I had to cut the whole lawn over again.

I canvassed the homes on our street and discovered several people needing their lawns mown and their gardens cared for. There I was just a few months from the asphalt and red brick neighbourhoods of South Philadelphia where no grass grew and had ever grown since Ben Franklin was in residence.

And there ere hedges to trim and I was kept busy.

My mother was inconsistent in her nagging. She'd go on about me for doing a better job on the lawns of my customers than I did on the patch around our house. That meant, I "cared more about them than you do your own." she didn't prohibit me doing the work yet when I wanted to get a paper route she wouldn't allow it because: "the neighbours will think we had to put you to work because we need the money."

When it snowed, I was out looking to shovel people's sidewalks, after having, of course, shoveled ours.

At twelve, thirteen years old, I already had a work history. I helped out at my uncle Joe Verechio's luncheonette at the Fifth and Catherine Streets. I learned to make change and to make sandwiches, mainly hoagies and mortadella, prosciutto and provolone on a roll. Occasionally, if Joe wasn't around I practiced my skill at doing a round steak and manicotti sandwich on a roll, remembering to pull out some of the bread in the middle of the roll.

I liked to go with my father to Pat's Steaks on Passyunk Avenue, not only for the good food but to pick up some pointers.

About this time, age eight or nine, I began carrying bags for women after they'd shopped at the Acme Market, Eighth and Wolfe. There were always two or three of us waiting by the cash registers. All the women lived in the neighbourhood so it wasn't hard work unless the lady had several bags. There were no shopping carts then. We usually got ten cents for the chore, occasionally a quarter. A few times there were 'extras.' One days I was at the Acme with my friend Joey Segal. There was a neighbour of his who needed our help. Joey said to me, "It's the gypsy lady."

We took the bags to her house on the 2400 hundred block of Eighth Street and she asked us to come in the house and put the bags in the kitchen. I'd never been in such a house. There paintings and rugs on the wall and a colourful carpet. There were lamps with scarves over the shades. The house smelled funny, not unpleasant just mysterious. The lady confessed that she had no money to give us but would make a cup of tea. Joey and I exchanged dissatisfied looks.

She gave us each our cup of tea and invited us to sit down the sofa that was covered with a shawl. She sat between us. It felt strange having her there, our thighs touching. The record she had put on also was strange.

We weren't sitting there more than five minutes before she put her hands on our thighs. Her right hand on Joey her left on me. She pulled down our flies and pulled found our penises. She tickled them and massaged them with her fingers. She did this slowly at first but soon was working faster and faster. It felt good. She took her hand off Joey and reached under her skirt. I saw the movement under there, like a little animal overed with cloth. I felt a funny sensation in my penis and after a minute Joey squealed.

When I got out of there, I knew something had changed and that the world was indeed a strange place with things going on that weren't apparent.

When I turned eleven, I graduated to shining shoes out front of the Trocadero Burlesque theatre at Eighth and Arch Streets in Philadelphia, I had been scouting locations while practicing my technique at home. I acquired a red shoeshine box with a grooved foot rest. The grooves kept the customer's shoe from slipping if he turned. This was especially important given my chosen location. In my reconnaissance I noticed that the door to the Troc didn't close all the way until the joint was locked and chained at night, and through the crack in the doorway you could see a sliver of stage and a woman going about her business. I positioned myself so the door was to my back and my box in front of me. The foot wide opening was a godsend for my business. A customer could watch a woman disrobing while getting his shoes shined. This way he didn't have to look like a cheap creep by just standing and staring. I made out like a bandit. And there were added benefits. Some of the girls took a liking to me and invited me to visit them in the dressing room. There was a bar on the corner called Leon's and some of the performers, there were also comedians and talkers, hung out at Leon's before and after shows.

I became a sort of mascot at in the joint and the boss occasionally gave me a watered-down glass of red wine that he made in the basement. "Direct from the hills of Puglia," he'd say.

Leon's was filled with characters. Like baseball George a one-time minor league ball player who had his major league dreams shot down at Guadacanal.

Another regular was a guy everyone called Frankie. He was convinced he looked and sounded like Frank Sinatra. He looked about as much like Sinatra as did the blond Tab Hunter who was big at the time. And he could not sing at all. He tried though, if he'd had enough to drink. He dressed in black suits always wore a skinny black tie and a stingy brim fedora. When inspired. Frankie would assume his position at the middle of the square of hardwood called the dance floor and go into his routine. He'd undo the top button of his white shirt, loosen his tie and start on a well-known song favoured by his idol. This could be something like, "Lover, Where Have You Been" or 'The Lady Is a Tramp" but his big number was "Old Black Magic."

Frankie was dead serious. His delusion was of such proportions that nobody made fun of him and no one dared laugh. Should a stranger drift in, catch Frankie act and make fun of him. He wouldn't have been able to walk out of there.

I shined Frankie's shoes a few times and he encouraged me to level with him about his abilities. I always told him he was wonderful and that, if I closed my eyes, I would swear it was The Man himself.

Occasionally—I was recruited to walk a girl home. The big time-strippers were on a circuit and were put up in hotels. Virginia 'Ding Dong' Belle who was advertised as possessing the measurements of 48-23-38, was the stripper I most often accompanied. The idea being that guys would be reluctant to hassle her with a kid in tow, or in front. She always made me walk in front of her because, she declared, she was liable at any moment to fall forward.

The hostelry most often selected for the girls was, I swear, The Biltmore.

So, there I was twelve years old, earning decent money shining shoes in front of burlesque house, taken up by the strippers and hanging out at a saloon filled with characters and I was suddenly wrenched from his ideal existence by my parent's announcement that we were moving to the suburbs.

I hated the place from the very moment we pulled up in back of the moving van in Springfield. I was there six years and my feeling about it never changed.

I mowed lawns and shovelled snow to keep myself occupied. I even began to paint cars. I spent much too much time on each one, often sanding it down to metal before spraying on a primer coat followed by the top coat. Once doing a 1954 Pontiac, there was an air leak in the compressor hose and before I knew it, the Pontiac had a dark green surface that looked as if the paint had been put on top of sand. I thought the effect was interesting but I assumed the customer would not agree. Much to my surprise, he didn't mind. In fact, he gave the old thing fender skirts, chrome hubcaps with spinners and whitewall tires, and told people it was a custom job.

I was not popular in school since I was known as the hoodlum kid from South Philadelphia. Therefore, I had no dates and wasn't permitted to play on any teams.

As soon as I turned sixteen, I got my driver's license and my first regular job, stocking shelves and driving a Volkswagen delivery van for a local drugstore. That wasn't a bad job, it provided me the opportunity to acquire some proficiency with a standard transmission, and there was oen significant perk. She was named Mrs. Sanderson. It all started the day I made my second delivery to her house where she lived alone. She gave me a look that I knew as meaningful but I was too naïve to know in what way. The second time I called at her home with the white bag of pills she invited me in and I wound up staying for an hour or so.

The experience was repeated a few more times.

One day back at the drugstore when Mr. Greenberg handed me a bag for Mrs. Sanderson, he said, "It seems like she's becoming a bit of a hypochondriac," And he looked into my eyes and nodded.

Mr. Greenberg was a short pudgy man with what were called liver spots up and down his arm and all over his bald head.

He probably wanted to be taken seriously as an important businessman and pillar of the community but he was just too funny looking albeit in a pleasant way. I thought he should be on the shelf with the fluffy ducks and teddy bears.

The experiences with Mrs. Sanderson and the gypsy woman (who might actually have been a beatnik) are the only sexual experiences I ever had during work although there were a couple of close calls. Funny for me to realize they both happened before I was seventeen years old. I've heard other guys, particularly landscapers, tell about their adventures with the lady of house. Not me, and I had other kinds of jobs that had me calling at houses in the afternoon and knocking on doors at all hours of the day and night. I was a census taker in a Pennsylvania town for two seasons, a landscaper in four states, three Canadian provinces and in the Yukon Territory. I just did the work.

There was one exception but it turned out to be a part of the job, and actually expected. I'll get to that later.

Forty years after Mrs. Sanderson, landscaping again, I was working at a woman's house in a medium sized town in British Columbia. The home owner was an outgoing woman always joking around so when she started making sexual references I didn't take it seriously. :References", hell: she was frank and overt. One time, at a party she put her hand down my pants in front of the guests assembled in the kitchen. Once she told me, "It's been so long since I had any action my you-know-what has cobwebs around it."

Then there was the time I was on a ladder outside, painting a window frame on the second floor. It was a warm day and the window was open I saw that she had come to stand by the window. "I see," she said, "that your crotch seems to be looking in my window."

So saying. she pulled my fly down and fished out my penis., me pressing forward and holding tightly on to the ladder. She brought her head down but I pulled away as much as I was able. "Joan," I said. "Stop. I'm twenty feet up a damn ladder."

"Yeah, you're right. When you come, you'll jolt back and go over. Too bad."

When I'd finished painting, I climbed down and had packed away my supplies, she was nowhere to be found.

A year I left Greenberg's, I was working at a place called The Bazaar of All Nations, in Clifton Heights near Springfield. The businesses or stalls were inside a huge warehouse building set up to resemble an oriental bazaar. There were clothing stalls, snack shops, places that sold pots and pans and dishes and furniture. I made and sold caramel corn. I worked over two large copper pots, mixing in the caramel sauce and the popped corn, bagging the stuff and putting it out for sale. The chores weren't demanding and I was usually kept busy.

I would drive to the Bazaar and leave my '51 Chevy around back. I always had to take a moment for the odour that awaited when I opened the back door, an indefinable blend of cooking greases. I worked there for four months and went out with a girl who was a karate instructor. She promised not to hurt me. We'd park and listen to the radio. 'our favourite current song was Troy Shondell's "This Time We're Really Breaking Up."

I quit making caramel corn when the boss wanted to cut my already low hourly wage. My next job was at a restaurant in Swarthmore on the opposite side of Springfield. I was a dishwasher. There was another pearl diver, a white guy older than me who started talking about masturbation the first night I worked there. It wasn't jerking off in general he went on about but his own exploits. After a week or so of it, I told him to change the subject. He didn't like that at all. I saw him a few days later in hushed conversation with the owner.

Clint was a tall man with short curly grey hair who was always chewing gum with his mouth open. He thought this was cool. Clint rarely ventured into the kitchen but it was my misfortune to be upgraded to busboy which put me in contact with him on the floor. He usually had something to say about a female patron, like "Check out the broad at table six. Look at the knockers on her." To which I'd reply, "Uh huh."

He'd also tell dirty jokes. I still remember one that he thought was hilarious. "How do you tell if a girl is old enough?"

"I don't know, Clint."

You put her in a barrel and if her head sticks up over the top, she's old enough. If it doesn't stick up, you know what you do?"

"No. what, Clint?"

"Saw the barrel in two."

When I didn't laugh, he asked, "What's the matter? Don't you have a sense of humour?"

From then on things were tense around the place. I got dirty looks from Clint and the jerk off in the kitchen.

Finally, I resigned my position.

Although twelve years would pass before I washed dishes at the Spanish restaurant in St. Augustine, it wasn't my last stint at a restaurant or washing dishes.

After high school, I went down to Virginia in June and a few months later found work at A. B. Ford's Amoco station outside the gates of Fort Lee. My parents had met there during the war when it was still called Camp Lee. My father was a private and my mother a secretary. In the time between graduation and the gas station I had a couple of short-lived jobs. The first was at a restaurant in Colonial Heights just north of Petersburg. Although most all history around there concerned the Civil War or what, below Mason-Dixon was known as the War Between the States, Colonial Heights derived its name from the Revolutionary War when Lafayette positioned his troops in the surrounding hills and fired down on the British.

I often wished he was still up there and would take care of some of the idiots who hassled me at the restaurant. I was hired to wait on customers who pulled up outside. I'd see a car, hustle out, take the order and bring it back out to them. The customers were mostly teenagers in their Daddies' cars and they'd try to impress their girl friends by making fun of my accent or asking me what was the matter with me, working a girl's job. This one flat-topped creep went through the same routine on three or four occasions, each time with a different girl friend. Finally, I invited him to step out of the car and find out if there was something the matter with me. He said, "I have her with me. I'll be back by myself."

He never showed.

The owner, a little guy with a dyed black moustache and a fringe of black hair in the vicinity of his ears, gave me added chores to do. So, there I was bussing table and sweeping up between dashing out to cars and back. Not surprisingly he didn't increase my salary.

I quit and put in a few days at the Brown and Williamson plant in Petersburg before starting at the Amoco station.

I liked this job, gassing up cars, changing oil and getting the vehicles up on the hydraulic lift for minor repairs and lubes.

I also had to change tires and patch inner tubes. To fix flats, I worked a heavy old metal apparatus that resembled some sort of medieval weapon or torture instrument. The tire went over a thick column and onto a broad platform. You used an iron bar like a long thick crow bar that rotated on the column. You pried the tire off the rim by wedging the business end of the bar between the rubber tire rim and the metal stand that seated the tire. Then you rotated the bar so it lifted the tire edge. It was necessary to grease the rubber edge so it wouldn't shred. After You repaired the tube, by inflating it and dipping it into a tub of water to find the puncture which you circled with a yellow marker, then dried and glued on a rubber patch after which the tube was inserted back into the tire, placed on the rack and you repeated the process with the iron bar.

Working the lift was always a bit tenuous. I could never believe that the hydraulics would really get the vehicle up in the air. The shafts had holes drilled into them and I had to insert a metal peg into the hole when the vehicle got aloft. I never completely trusted these to keep the two or three thousand pounds from crashing down. For some reason, however, it didn't seem as ominous when I was underneath the vehicle. The place was owned by a guy named A. B. Ford. He adhered to all the prerequisites for red neck-ism but was moderate in expressing his views. For instance, he never used the 'N. word unlike his only other employee, a wiry dark complected fellow with a prominent Adam's Apple named Harold. He had an oily brown pompadour and worked the four to midnight shift. He was never late and we always exchanged a few words or, rather I listened to him. Harold would look over the cars and pickup trucks that had been brought in during my shift and needed work. He'd open the door of each one, sniff the interior and pronounce the race of the driver. "White," he'd say. "Nigger . . . nigger. . . white" The infuriating thing was that he was never wrong. At first, I thought maybe he was familiar with the cars but, no, he'd go through his routine with cars he'd never seen before, brought in by soldiers new to the base.

I became friendly with one of the soldiers, an Italian guy who already served a tour in Vietnam and was haunted by his memories. Of course, America troops were only supposed to be there as advisors. This was the summer of 1963. But the soldier told me of taking Vietnamese up in helicopters, questioning them and pushing them out the doors. Later. I'd hear similar stories that parents, politicians and other patriots always denied. "Americans would never do that." Many years later in the war museum in Hanoi, I saw photos of it being done.

My Italian friend was haunted and ashamed at being a part of such a thing. Before the summer ended, I was dead set against the war and my opinion never changed. Back in Springfield I was offered a good job at the Vertol helicopter plant, a company formerly known as Piasecki Helicopter, just over the town line in Morton but I turned it down. When the foreman or boss or whatever he was wanted to know why I'd do such a stupid thing, I made the mistake of telling him. I had been a high school greaser and outsider and now I'd started along the road to being an anti-American Commie.

I began college at West Chester State in Pennsylvania. That first attempt at higher education was short-lived. The classes were easier than high school. I had a philosophy course where the teacher, who looked like a walrus that had just rolled out of bed, slumped at his desk and read from the philosophy text book in a weary monotone.

The best part of that one semester was my job in the shipping-receiving department. I worked with an older fellow, maybe fifty, who was a dead ringer for Henry Miller. His name was Arnold but I called him Henry. He never objected and always responded to the name.

There wasn't much to ship or receive but I had my hours to fill so I got a lot of reading done. I'd make myself comfortable on a wide wooden bench; meanwhile Arnold who had even less to do, slept on another wide wooden bench. I thought of him recently when my pal Stu Young told me about an older man he worked with in a warehouse in Calgary. This guy slept most of his shift wrapped in blankets on planks laid across hot water pipes

That first stint at higher education ended one morning during the class called Middle Eastern Politics. The professor said, "The first thing you have to understand is that the Arabs are the cause of all the problems." He added something about the great democratic nation of Israel. After I ascertained he was serious I stood up and walked out of class and a few days later got out of West Chester. I tossed a gym bag of clothes and toiletries, a hot plate and an immersion heater, and a few books into the back seat of my '54 Ford and was gone. I drove west through relatively little-known parts of Pennsylvania and Maryland before turning south.

I didn't stop until I reached Memphis. There I got a temporary job, a two-week job—on the docks, shifting around boxes and heavy burlap sacks full of grain. I rented a room with a little window that looked out over the Mississippi. At night I cooked up rice and bacon and beans on my hot plate and was not unhappy.

None of the people I worked with were particularly interesting, no unappreciated bluesmen having to tear themselves away from their art to feed themselves and pay the rent.

When my two weeks were up, I got some work at shape-ups on the dock, spent part of a week working the grill in a greasy spoon and then I headed back to Pennsylvania. There I moved back in with my parents and found an actual decent job as Junior Clerk with the Philadelphia Electric Company in their headquarters at Tenth and Chestnut Streets in Philadelphia.

As sort of a glorified Messenger boy. I was stationed on the executive floor and did errands for the Chairman of the Board, the President, the Executive Vice-President and their secretaries. I surprised myself by liking the job and the people I worked for. They liked me too. One afternoon, I shared an elevator with the chairman of the board. He wore rimless glasses and a blue pin-striped shirt. He noticed the book I was carrying, Homer's The Iliad, and began reciting passages from it in the original Greek. We were talking happily away about it when one of the executive secretaries got on the elevator. When we reached the bottom floor the Chairman said my name as he went his way. I imagined news of our chat spread as fast as the elevator could travel. It turns out that the Chairman rarely spoke a word to the lowly workers. I was treated differently after that.

Much of my chores consisted of taking a mail trolley around, delivering messages, making copies and fetching coffee but I also spent a lot of time outside the building, entire days sometimes. I went to purchase train or airline tickets and got to be a regular visitor to the Union Club on Broad Street. A few times, took a taxi or rode the company limousine to the airport to pick up a visitor. One of these times, the visitor was the English actor, Jean Simmons. She was making an appearance at Wanamaker's, the classiest of the city's department stores. Gene Simmons stood by the perfume counter on behalf of one brand or another. My job was to stand three feet away and protect her. Every now and again, she'd catch my eye and make a face, as if to say, "How'd I ever get involved in something this ridiculous!"

She was beautiful, unlike anyone I'd ever seen before. When I thought of the best-looking women I'd ever seen, those others might have belonged to another species entirely. After the Wannaker's chore I accompanied her to the hotel where she was staying. When she invited me in for a drink, I thought, So, this is what it means to go weak in the knees. We had the drink and I got out of there, the only time I had or ever would have that feeling. I was in awe of her and had to get out of there. Callow and naïve, I know I was.

My work mates came and went. There was a tall, skinny fellow my age, nineteen whose main topic of conversation was his retirement plans. He was going to open a fishing camp in New Jersey and figured he'd be done with the electric company by the time he was forty-two. Did his dream ever come true?

More interesting to me anyway was a black guy, also my age, named Clarence. He wasn't an engineer therefore he had two strikes against him. He dressed in the Ivy League manner which was known as Conserve. We got along well and had lunches together which was still an unusual thing to do. Like me he had been born in Richmond, Virginia, and when after a year I quit Philadelphia Electric, I told him I'd be heading south. He gave me his girl cousin's phone number and dared me to look her up. I did too.

The messenger job was also a way station for linemen who had been injured on the job. They were able to do errands and non-demanding chores. Most of them were twenty or so years older than me and the others.

There was a white metal, glass fronted box near our desk. When we were summoned, there'd be a click and a metal flag would stand up. The number on the flag indicated which office wanted us.

At lunch time when I didn't pal around with Clarence, I checked out the two newsstands in the neighbourhood. One of them also sold paperback books. In one or the other of these I was sure to see an overweight, middle-aged man in a wrinkled suit looking through books or magazines about baseball. He'd be absorbed in albums of statistics which I'm sure he knew already. That's probably why he came back to them over and over. Willie Mays would forever rob Wertz of that extra base hit in the world series. Bob Feller would always have that great rookie year. Ted Williams always bat 401.

Another thing that never changed was that the man always looked weary and defeated. I conjured all sorts of stories for him, He had a bad home life, his wedding ring seemed to be shrinking on his finger. He hated his job and dragged himself though the notions every day before going home to a nasty wife and unruly kids. His only escape was these magazine stores where he lost himself in baseball dreams. I gradually stopped calling at the shops because he reminded me of what I might become if I kept denying what I really wanted to do which was to go out and see a bit of the world.

Instead of the shops I might head over to the Mercantile branch of the public library which was just across Chestnut Street. I'd look at maps or scan the shelves trying to decide what to borrow. Besides the predictable Hemingways and Fitzgeralds, I went through some unlikely stuff for a fellow relatively new to the world of books, I read Thomas Hardy and Willa Cather. Even A. J. Cronin. I liked James T. Farrell and Willard Motley and Wright Morris. Whenever I couldn't decide I'd take out a John Steinbeck and he rarely disappointed.

Later, I discovered that the fascinating and irascible Sadakichi Hartman used to spend his own lunch times in the same Mercantile branch.

The trouble with this midday reading was I had to stop it and return to my job, my head filled with interesting people and far away places. Like I said, I didn't mind the job, I just wanted to be somewhere else.

I stayed at Philadelphia Electric for exactly a year, the longest continuous full-time employment I would ever have. I resigned to do what I fantasized about. To see some of the world. What I saw at first was the inside of a Greyhound bound for Orlando, Florida. We pulled into the Orlando station at three in the morning. The freeway approach to the city was so disheartening that I only got off long enough to purchase a through ticket to Miami. It was fortunate that I did because I met a fellow my age from Southern Illinois named Val Santee. He would become my closet friend. We hung out together in Miami Beach, taking a room in a South Beach rooming house operated by a man who had been an alligator wrestler before winning a pile at the nearby dog track. Val and I pursued our own interests. I thought our friendship had come to a brief end when he disappeared.

    I got a job as a dishwasher at a well-known seafood restaurant on Ocean Drive. The dishes were done at three sinks in a tiny room at the back of the place. It was sweltering in there without even a fan. There was a screen door but never even the hint of a breeze.

    The boss was an Italian who acted like he was connected, maybe he was. One night the man next to me who was red faced and had been breathing heavily, collapsed. I called the boss and told him an ambulance was needed. He prodded the man with the toe of one black wingtip shoe. I can still he his gauzy black silk sock.

    I found scraping off and washing those plates disgusting; there was grease and food scraps and pieces of lobster shell and stone crab smeared over plates in a skein of tartar sauce, and a top coat of coffee. But this was pristine kitchen work compared to that of my buddy Alan Sirulnikoff who worked in the University of British Columbia Hospital kitchen in intense heat and noise from machinery, and surrounded by fellow workers from Ghana, Pakistan and the Philippines.

    He dressed in full kitchen battle garb: white dietary clothing, plastic apron, rubber boots, mask and ear plugs. He needed it.

    The worst place in the kitchens was the dish room, Alan said, with the familiar plastic trays of left over food. These were tossed into a sluice of fast running water; the food spewed out was ground up and disposed of as garbage.

    But Alan put up with it because the pay was good and he had trips to take.

    Back in that kitchen in the Miami Brach seafood joint, the owner was standing over the passed out dishwasher hollering, "Get up

Ya bum!""

"He's not going to get up without some help," I told him.

"Then give me some help tossing him out back."

"You mean you're not going to call an ambulance?"

"What for? He's just some old wino. An ambulance showing up would be bad for business."

"Well, I'm going to call."

"You ain't using one of my phones."

"He's liable to die."

"What are you, some bleeding heart?"

"Yeah, and I'm going across the street and make a call."

"You leave your sink, you don't come back."

"It's a deal."

And that was it for that job.

I next hired as a factotum at one of the small art deco hotels on Ocean Drive. When I went to the interview, the manager gave me a careful once over that had me thinking he was a homosexual (the word 'gay' wasn't used in that context in 1964).

I had to serve drinks around the pool and do a little clean up. I also was required to make minor repairs in the rooms. My second day on duty, the woman whose sink I unclogged, slithered up to me and began to grind her hips into my crotch. Well, I wondered about neglected my official duties but I was also nineteen years old and she was attractive and no more that fifteen years older. We proceeded to mess around; the woman glanced at the window and down at the pool to see if her husband was still sitting in his plastic chair, reading the Wall Street Journal like the rest of them. My vision of them is of all these men in bathing suit trunks. Hairy legs, white strip of sunscreen on their noses that were buried in the newspaper while upstairs their wives were carrying on with the kid who fixed the sink.

I was two hours on that chore and when I got down to the office, figured my employment was terminated. But it was worth it, I told myself, and jobs weren't hard to find.

But no; when I went into the office, the manager just nodded his head and smirked, and I immediately realized why he had given me the onceover.

I was at the hotel for a month and it wasn't the last time, I got involved in that kind of escapade. One day Val Santee showed up and to explain his absence, mumbled something about the Fair Play for Cuba Committee. I said, "Man, you'll never believe the job I have."

I figured I could get him on but He wasn't interested. He wanted to get on the road so we did, hitchhiking. It was a great trip that included three days with a hillbilly couple in a '51, Mission sleeps a couple of night and in a wrecking yard near Nahunta, Georgia. The hillbillies had no money and we didn't have much ourselves. It didn't matter because they had a little game to run down. The girl Marie was fourteen years old and visibly pregnant. When food or gas or a tire was needed, we would locate a local preacher whether at his home or at his church. Pete and Marie would approach the man and. if he was a Methodist, tell him they were Methodists themselves and just trying to get home to North Carolina where they had jobs writing at the local textile mill.

If the preacher man was Episcopalian, so were they. We had to make these visits at least twice a day, the car had bald tires and shot bearings and belched blue spirals of smoke.

After Val and I witnessed the first couple preachers being hit up, Marie, the boss, informed us we'd have to get with it to it to pay for our ride. I went first, a little shy about my southern accent. but I must have passed because we were successful. Marie stood looking sadly at the man and rubbing her protruding belly. I mention all this because it was work of a sort.

It took us four days to get to Nahunta, Georgia by which time Val and I were both sick of their bickering. We left Pete and Marie at a garage in town staring up at the underside of the Studebaker. We continued our hitch hiking.

Jobs were all over the place in those days. We got out of a car near a construction site on the highway outside Rocky Mount, North Carolina, approached the works and were immediately hired. Val carried lumber and I mostly loaded wheel barrows with sand and pushed them where needed.

After that we made our way north to Petersburg and I put in another few days at Brown and Williamson and Val got on at pouring fibreglass into moulds at a boat building place. I also worked a few days at Sealtest after the boss man measured the circumference of my wrists. After two weeks of it, we continued north to Philadelphia. After hanging around for awhile with my pal Bobby Garzarelli on the University of Pennsylvania campus, Val did another of his disappearing acts.
I was busy that great year if 1965. I roamed the country and down and into Mexico, worked a dozen casual jobs and even got married to a woman I'd known for five days.

In Chicago, I went to see all the sites that had to do with the Wobblies. I was surprised to learn there was an IWW headquarters. the organization still in operation. I got my red card then I got on the road to Kansas City. There I was walking around the stockyard area one afternoon when I stopped in a greasy spoon for lunch. I heard old men talking about anarchism and the Spanish Civil War.

The restaurant was full and the man behind the counter was being run ragged. I head him tell someone that his Grille man hadn't shown up. I stood up, went around the counter. Grabbed an apron and shot him a look. He nodded and I picked up the next order from a hook on the vent.

Sometimes over the next two weeks I worked so fast time seemed to just fly by. My shift would end just when I thought I was getting in the groove. I loved that joint with all those radical workmen. I never knew who I'd be serving a coffee and a sinker. It might be some old pal of Joe Hill or T-Bone Slim. They were of a breed that had entirely ceased to exist before five years had passed.

The owner finally hired a likely looking grille man who vowed to stay on for the duration. I backed away and kept on going west.

Soon, I got a ride to Manhattan, Kansas and was in a service station buying a snack when a redheaded fellow who just filled his tank, asked me if I knew anything about construction work.

"A little."

"Good I got two weeks work for you if you want it."

I did and he put me to it framing and banging nails on a small piece of land at a cul de sac in a budding development. At night, I'd unroll my sleeping bag on the floor of one or the other of the houses. My employer brought me lunches and sometimes we got dinner together, usually at a barbecue restaurant.

We often worked at the same house and when we were done at the sites, he said he'd probably have some more work for me in a week or so if I wanted it.

I almost regretted not sticking around but the wanderlust proved stronger.

I got a ride out of Manhattan in a new black Cadillac with a man who looked like book jacket photos I'd seen of the novelist, Robert Ruark. He assured me that was not who he was. He was a rugged, sharply-dressed man, unusual for a white man in America. I would later come across men in Europe like that. He had invented some kind of revolutionary new central heating system. Two bodyguards followed him in another black Cadillac.

After an hour or so, the man pulled over to let me out. The other Cadillac pulled up behind us. As we stood on the side of the road, the man gave me a matchbook cover on which he had written the name of a fellow in San Francisco who could help me get on a ship. The body guards closely watched this transaction and our goodbye handshake.

I admit to feeling a bit lonesome there in all that crepuscular Kansas vastness. In the distance I spotted a black shape coming perpendicular to the highway. After a few minutes, I recognized it as a car. Then I saw it was a small dark green automobile. A Triumph convertible, as a matter of fact. Then it was being driven by a young woman. She got to the highway junction a few minutes before me and watched me come along.

When I was close enough to be heard, I asked her if she'd give me a ride, not expecting that she would.

"Hop in," she said.

The top was down and there was too much wind to be heard clearly but I got across the fact that I was headed to California.

I thought her a stunning woman with her thick wavy dark hair and fine features. Her skirt ended an inch above her knee, just enough to be provocative. We came to a crossroads and she pulled over.

"I'm turning south. I live on the Mexican border."

"I'll get out then, I'm heading for San Francisco."

She didn't reply for a moment, just looked at me and finally asked, "Have you ever been to Mexico?"

"Nope. Never."

"You want to go?"

"Yes."

It took us four days to get to her little town and her little yellow house. We stayed together in motel rooms and listened to country music on the radio while tractor trailers roared by in the night.

I had never had feelings remotely like what I felt for her from the very beginning. She told me she felt the same way. Family pressures, the intended's and hers, conspired to keep us apart. She had grown up in the town where she lived in East Texas; it was no western town but a southern one with all the narrow-minded, right wing racism that signifies.

She was miserable at the thought of marrying the guy but couldn't go against her mother's will. The estranged father was all for Linda Louise and I tying the knot or living in sin as long as we took off for parts unknown and left that narrow minded burg behind.

We had six weeks of something like bliss. Then we had to face the inevitability of what we both knew had to happen.

For five of those six weeks Linda Louise returned to her job in a small office on the main drag, North Pearl Street. Sometimes I'd walk by and look up at the second-floor window hoping to catch a glimpse of her through the pane.

I had become friendly with the brother of a priest we'd encountered. It turns out Nestor was part owner of a high-class brothel on the Mexican side. He told me that business wasn't so great. I replied that I knew how to increase his business.

There was a two-year college on the American side and it had to be filled with horny young males. The sexual revolution hadn't reached east Texas yet. I proposed bringing car loads of college boys to the brothel, called La Abrugada.

He liked the idea but, I said, the only thing lacking is the vehicle to transport them. He had two Plymouths, a two-year old model and a big heavy old 1948 four door sedan. He handed me the keys to the two-year old car but I handed them back. "I want the other one."

"What are you crazy! That's a short for un Viejo. Why the hell do you want that one?"

"It has character."

"Character!"

Also, it can carry more kids.

I made myself known at the two-year college, extolled the virtues of the girls and women who operated there. I never said 'worked.' Of eight girls, five were Mexicans, one negro and two whites, a young one and an older one, at least thirty-five. The young white blonde earned the most money but the Mexican connoiseurs preferred the oldest of the Mexican women because she was supposed to know certain secrets. My deal with Nestor was that I got five dollars for every kid I brought over. When my total amounted to five I would take cash or have a session with a girl. I was in love with a beautiful woman, I took the money. The town where Linda Louise was born and raised was an East Texas town, a southern town not a western one. It was a typical small-minded right wing racist place. Her mother pressured her constantly to ditch the drifter boy friend and 'pray to God'—she actually put it that way—that the air force guy would take her back. She called her daughter L.L. which irritated me.

Linda Louise didn't want to marry the guy, she wanted to run away with me. Her father who lived in Port Arthur and had nothing to do with the mother, encouraged Linda Louise to make the break and do just that. We visited him at his work one day and he told her if she went through with her planned marriage she'd regret it for the rest of her life.

To underscore the mother's opposition, as if that was needed, she came around the house one afternoon and shot me. Linda Louise and I were goofing around me in shorts and her in a bathing suit taking turns to spray each other with a garden house and stopping now and again for kisses.

Then the mother appeared from around the side of the house, expression grim and determined. I knew something unpleasant was in the works, and assumed she was preparing for another harangue. But there was something about the way she held her handbag in front of her. She was staring at me and her hand went into the bag. I was standing next to the wall of the cinder block garage. Then the gun appeared; I recall thinking how small and harmless it looked. I know nothing about guns put was later told it was a short barrel .38.

I instinctively moved to my left and she fired. The bullet missed me by a couple of inches but I caught its ricochet on my lower back, right side and was sprayed by shrapnel from the soft the soft cinder block.

The women screamed at each other and the mother got herself out of there. My back burned and if I touched the wounds I got stabbing needles of pain.

I knew I needed to get help but couldn't go to the hospital because they'd have to report the incident to the police. Linda Louise called Nestor who got hold of a doctor on the Mexican side. He was waiting when we showed up. I lay face down on a cot and the doctor began taking out bits of cinder using rubbing alcohol and tweezers. I think there was some of the other kind of alcohol put on my wounds. I know I was given a couple drinks of it, Mescal, my first tastes of the stuff and I've liked it ever since.

When it came down to it Linda Louise couldn't go against her mother's wishes. A week after I was shot, we were at the beach on a beautiful afternoon. It was called Baghdad. She had a transistor radio and we were listening to the Beach Boys. Linda Louise liked them and I pretended to.

She stopped running her hands through the sand and turned off the radio, looked at me with tears in her eyes, and I knew what she was going to say.

After she said it, she kissed my lower back. I still have the pinpoint scars.

I left the next day. She urged me to stay but I couldn't face it. At the bus station, the clerk asked me where I wanted to go, I looked at the battered map of Texas on the wall and said Beaumont.

When I got there it was late afternoon, I walked out onto the street and there were men in seersucker suits and women in cotton summer dresses with sensible shoes. I leaned against a lamppost and gave a gander to the main stem. Across the way I noticed a man who did not look like the rest of them. He had a sunburned, weathered face, wearing a Hawaiian shirt and smoking a black stogie. His hair was long and grey with a yellow tint to it like it used to be blond. I figured he had to be in his fifties.

I went over to meet him because it was people like I sensed him to be that I'd gone out to find.

His name was Floyd Wallace and right away, I realized he would have been sitting on a stool in the greasy spoon in Kansas City cutting up touches with Joe Hill.

When he recognized that I wasn't running down any game and knew who Emma Goldman and even Carlo Tresca were, he accepted me and we decided to strike out together. In fact, he was looking for someone to help him at a construction job in Beaumont. He'd been hired a couple of days earlier but the boss couldn't find any one else who wanted to work.

It seems that every where I went in those days, a job was waiting whether I was looking for one or not. Floyd knew the widow of an old Wobbly buddy who let him stay in her boarding house. I went along and got my own room. I started work the next morning.

The foreman left the site at one point and another employee took advantage of his absence to stop working. He lay down on a sand pile but stirred himself enough to hassle Floyd about continuing to work. Floyd replied that he'd been hired to do a job and was doing it. The guy told him he must be a boss's man and added something about being in with the capitalists.

Not a good thing to say to an old Wobbly.

"I'm doing what I said, I'd do," Floyd told him.

The man summoned the energy to get up from his sand pile and took a step toward Floyd. I thought they were going to go at it but the man suddenly found something of interest in his discarded shovel. Floyd became my hobo mentor. After the Beaumont job we went out to Denver to meet up with an old girl friend of his who sang country in a tavern in the foothills.

After a week we headed back east to the hobo convention at Britt, Iowa. We hit town riding a box car and jumped down not far from where the Bos had cook fires going in 40-gallon oil drums.

There were still old-times hobos then, some men in their early Seventies who had been riding freights fifty years before there were diesel locomotives. Most of the guys had nicknames that they'd earned. There was the Pennsylvania Kid, Scoop Shovel Scotty and Frisco Jack. I'm sure I met the legendary Lord Open Road that year, a man I'd get to know later.

It was the hobos who opened up the west and Midwest and had such an impact on agricultural development. They rode freights, following the harvest from one job to another and were known as boomer workers. Had they not done so there would have been no one to harvest the corn and pick the fruit and, thus, no fruit or corn to sell.

Floyd knew all these people and they all knew him. Of course, there was plenty of reminiscing about trains and who had recently caught a westbound and did you know that Sally the good-looking key in Modesto went and got hitched to Liberty Earl. The latter was not to be confused, Floyd assured me, with his old friend High Rigger Earl.

Earl, according to Floyd, had a face like an old boot which I thought described his own mug. When they paled around together, Earl was thirty years older than Floyd just as Floyd was thirty years older than me.

Earl was a high rigger in circuses as opposed to theatres. He had to give up work when it became too difficult to get up on the high beams. Later, Earl's health wouldn't allow him to hop freights. When Floyd was with him, they tramped across country only taking rides when they were offered.

At night they'd make a fire, cook up some 'grub' as Floyd called it and tell stories, at least Earl told stories. He had some good ones, too. He started on the bum back at the end of the last century. He was a Wobbly and got with the International Brigades in Spain. Afterwards he just continued knocking around getting work when he could find some.

He'd talk about all that and about the characters he met along the way. This one-night Earl said he was 'plumb tuckered out and tired of his own voice. Why didn't I tell a tale for a change."

They drank coffee from those speckled tin cups that used to be just the thing for campers and anyone who slept out.

"I told a story. I think it was about shipping out on the Murmansk run but it didn't get any response so I went into one about the fighting on the Plains of Teruel. The country over there sort of resembled where we were which was near Norman, Oklahoma

"The fire crackled like ricochets. It was a pleasant night. I thought of how my cup resembled the night sky. But Earl wasn't moving a muscle and seemed to be absorbed by the fire, Probably thinking the kind of things that campfires provoke. I banged my cup against a rock but he didn't stir. Finally, I got up and went over to him but Earl was dead".

"What did you do?" I asked Floyd.

"I went through his pockets, looking for his red card. I took the card and the few dollars he had. If the powers-that-be found that card, Earl wouldn't even rate a pauper's grave. As for the three or four dollars, no sense some scissor bill having it.

"There was nothing to do but move on. I walked toward the plains of Norman and thought about those of Teruel."

Everyone was surprised by the appearance of one particular attendee that year, the elusive Seldom Seen Slim.

When the Bos weren't talking about trains, they recalled jobs the trains had taken them to, sometimes on fish boats in Maine or in logging camps in Oregon and Washington State but more often the work was not picturesque at all. They were jobs such as I had been doing.

After the convention I headed east figuring on going back to Philadelphia to find something. My forward or backward motion came to a halt not long after it started. I had gone to a matinee show in Sioux City featuring Blackstone the magician. Afterwards I was picked up for vagrancy. I had been standing outside the theatre trying to decide whether to catch a bus or find the road out of town. The cops called it loitering. I showed them money but their object was to bust me so they weren't going to be dissuaded in their desire to vag me.

The night judge didn't care either and gave me five days plus fine. I asked him if I was a vagrant how would I be able to pay the fine. He gave me two more days for talking back.

It wasn't bad, I had a clean cell and there was no cellmate to bother me. The Deputy was a good man and told me he knew I had been treated unfairly. He saw to it that I only served two and a half days. In the course of our conversations, it had came out that I was a landscaper. He told that his old mother lived by herself in a big house with a big yard. She liked to keep her yard neat and tidy but the fellow she usually hired to do the work had left town.

Now it was Autumn with no one to rake the leaves and put the garden to bed.

The deputy was too busy to do it what with his job and his own yard and kids. So, he let me out on the stipulation that I put in a few days for his mother. I did and went back to my cell to sleep at night. When I had gotten everything looking nice, the lady gave me a few dollars and a couple of apples.

I went and bought a bus ticket to Chicago. When I arrived. I immediately gave up plans to hitchhike and bought another ticket for Philadelphia. And there I was two days later in Media, Pennsylvania sleeping with my girl friend, Carolyn Trice in her parents four poster bed.

They were in Florida. After a couple of days, Carolyn drove me to Philadelphia in her parents' car, a white Cadillac convertible. Carolyn had once driven me to my parent's place and as she pulled away my mother said, "Your girl friend must be a whore to have a car like that."

The Horn and Hardarts restaurant chain originated in Philadelphia in the late 1800s. These eateries were usually huge places with cafeteria lines but the big attraction was the pies and cakes and sandwiches that you could see in compartments with glass windows. If you wanted what was in there, you inserted the appropriate coin, turned the brass knob and took out your food. Many years later, in Dawson City, Yukon, at the post office that had been in operation since Gold Rush days, I saw compartments with brass fittings just like the ones at Horn and Hardarts. They were smaller and you didn't have to pay a quarter and turn a round knob to retrieve the contents. There were, incidentally, letters in those Dawson City slots that had lain there unclaimed since '98.

When I proved capable of filling the slots, I was put to work toting hot food in metal trays from the kitchen to the steam counter. I didn't like fitting the trays into the appropriate openings because it was too easy to get burned. Taking the empties out was even worse. I was happy to be promoted from the line to the grille where I was soon making breakfasts. Sometimes six of them at once. Eggs anyway you wanted them with bacon or sausage and sometimes steak. I learned a lot about this work from a grille man who was a ringer for Bo Diddley. He and the waitresses of a certain vintage communicated in old-time restaurant talk. "Two on a raft float 'em" or "Blind a pair with oars."

Unfortunately, the first outlet where I worked was a short block away from the Philadelphia Electric Company, and my old bosses came in to eat and made it obvious they felt sorry for me, sorry about how far I'd fallen.

After I'd been there for a month, Val showed up again. He'd been in Yonkers north of Manhattan selling magazine subscriptions door to door. I got him on at Horn and Hardarts but he only lasted a couple of weeks before disappearing again.

Fortunately, I got transferred to another outlet and another one after that. I felt like a utility infielder. I wound up at the restaurant in Lansdowne in Delaware County near Springfield.

The carnival came to town and left after three days, and I left with it. I was taken on as what they called a roughie. I did odd jobs, mainly helping to set up tents and tear them down again. I did a lot of stake pounding.

I started out as a lowly 'forty-mile wonder,' a guy who didn't go far away from home but I soon expanded my range. It was a great experience, a trade I would come back to several times over the years. I met special people, known as 'freaks,' but the word wasn't a prejorative. I was at the lowest level of the carnival, the freaks were at the top. I associated with pinheads and seven hundred pound ladies, with people covered by hair and individuals known then as half and halves. I signed on with various shows and got to know the alligator man and the great Francis O'Connor who was born without arms. She appeared in Todd Browning's 1934 movie *Freaks*.

There was a weekly trade newspaper called *Amusement Business* and it had a jobs available section. There might be an announcement that a 'ride boy (a kid to operate the merry-go-round or the tilt-a-whirl) was needed at Specialty Shows that would be in Kokomo, Indiana until May 29th. So off I'd go and try to make Kokomo in time to get on.

I made that particular show and found my lowly niche. A couple of weeks later in a place called French Lick, I was pulling up tent pegs next to Lamond Stoval, the Alligator Man, when the Townies showed up wielding their baseball bats.. There were a couple of guards hired to keep the locals off the lot but they must have been playing cards or dozing off under a truck or maybe they just looked the other way. I learned this kind of thing was not an infrequent occurrence.

In the minds of the Townies the strange carnival people were equated with Communists and other undesirables. Most of these rhubarbs were instigated by the American Legion and other service groups like the Lions and the Elks.

I got along just fine with Lamond. He was in his forties and had an advanced case of ichthyosis which caused his skin to dry up and form flakes which looked a lot like dark cornflakes. We had started off talking about western movies. He was glad to find someone who shared his passion for these films which he called dusters or oaters. He read western novels, too which I had little knowledge of. The first question he asked me was I suppose you know who the man was who shot Liberty Vallance?"

"Sure, and I know who played Liberty Vallance. Did you now that Williams S. Hart was a real cowboy?"

And on and on it went. I was pulling up tent pegs one afternoon with the alligator man when the townies showed up wielding crowbars and baseball bats. There were a couple of guards hired to keep the locals off the lot but they must have been playing cards or dozing off under a truck or maybe they just looked the other way.

I had picked up a copy of Amusement Business, the bible of show people, at a newsstand in Akron Ohio, and came across a notice indicating a roughie was needed, immediately, with Shaw-Daks Shows. The outfit's itinerary for the week was given and I figured I'd be able to catch them at the tear down in Kokomo, Indiana.

I set off right away but got nabbed almost immediately, in Canton, Ohio, for hitchhiking on the interstate. I had just gotten a ride down the Akron-Canton Corridor, as they called it, and it was a peculiar ride, indeed. Looking back, the whole experience is, well, if not exactly funny, certainly ridiculous.

So they nearly finished the tear down by the time I reached Kokomo. I helped with the tents and loaded gear and rode in the back of a truck during the run south to French Lick.

The set-up went well and the next evening I was on the bally assisting the talker in drawing a tip. It wasn't what I was hired for but the talker seemed to think I could turn a phrase so he had me stand to the side and toss in comments now and again. There was a half-and-half and a fire-eater/sword swallower; a fat woman and the alligator boy. His name was Lamond Stovall and he was by far the most popular attraction on the lot, save for the girl show.

The thing that made Lamond popular, as well as drawing the ire of some of the rednecks, was that he looked like he was one of them except for what was a virulent case of ichthyosis vulgaris. He skin was dry and scaly with large light brown scales that resembled nothing so much as flakes of breakfast cereal. He would appear in just his slacks and the yokels would stare open mouthed at his upper body. Leland always gave a little shake before disappearing behind the curtain, leaving a puddle of scales where he stood.

Later when I saw him taking a shower around back of the mess tent, I learned that the condition had not spared an inch of him. Standing there under the shower contraption, he resembled a large white and brown spotted fish standing on its tail fin.

He was a nice fellow, careful about his appearance. He trimmed his fingernails and his toenails, used Vitalis on his hair, parted it on one side and kept it cut short. When he wasn't performing, Leland could usually be found sitting in the shade of a truck or tent reading western novels or rubbing moisturizing lotion on his skin. He was very polite, too. It he went visiting he always swept up any scales he'd left behind.

He liked to talk about his western novels and about western movies which he called 'oaters' or 'dusters'. I hadn't read very many westerns although I did give Ernest Haycox a try, mainly because Kenneth Rexroth, a poet and essayist who I admired, had written that Haycox was a far more important writer than William Faulkner. A ludicrous statement but I came to suspect that Rexroth liked to see what he could get away with.

But I could hold my own with the Alligator Man when it came to oaters. He would try me with questions, like, "I guess you know who shot Liberty Vallance, don't you?"

Sure," I answered. "Did you know William S. Hart was a real cowboy?"

On and on it went.

We were working side by side, pulling up tent pegs after the run in Dubuque when the townies attacked and the "Hey Rube!" rang out. No one knew exactly what caused the fracas, not that Townies ever needed a reason. They hated the sideshow freaks and the operators, figuring none of either category could be decent people like they were. Maybe one of them developed funny feelings about Bobby/Bobbi the half-and-half or had a mild case of psoriasis and feared winding up like Leland the Alligator Man. Whatever the cause, they came with a vengeance wielding baseball bats and tire irons, some of them carrying American flags.

Most of the carnies engaged directly in the battle, others saw to getting the freaks into trailers and trucks because they were the operation's most valuable assets. The yokels no doubt told themselves they'd be striking a blow for America if they put the boots to a pinhead. Only Jenny the fat lady got into any hand to hand combat but the dwarf, Big Marty, used his cut-down bow and arrow from a perch on the roof of a Mack cab and protected by the rise of the trailer. The arrows were metal-tipped and effective.

It was quite a melee, bodies falling and rising all over the lot. The police showed up and hung about the edge of the lot doing little except to rescue a townie whenever one of them seemed to be getting the worst of it along the fringes.

The fighting was fierce; it seemed like it went on for an hour but probably only lasted twenty minutes and might have gone on longer except that someone set fire to the only tent that remained standing. The police jumped in to cordon off the area until the fire trucks showed up.

Not that they were protective of carnival property; no, there were trucks near the tent and a small shopping centre adjacent to the lots.

Leland and I replayed the Hey, Rube long after midnight, drinking cheap package store brandy around the fold-down table in his 17-foot trailer as we rolled west through the dark, Marshall One-Eye, the electrician, driving. I had a cut under my right eye and a fat lip but Leland had escaped injury, at least, injury to his body. If the insults bothered him, he didn't let on. Perhaps he was used to it; God knows he'd heard enough of them. Me, however, I was shocked at what people said to him, and to the other freaks.

That night we had our most intimate conversation. I didn't have much to reveal but Leland did. He told me horrible stories about growing up, his father and mother happily sending him off at the age of fourteen to the carnival after a sideshow operator gave them a sort of signing bonus. How he had a twin brother who was normal and lived in New York City.

Leland sent him money every month. "Not that he needs it because he has a good job and supports a wife and a child quite comfortably. I also send some to my mother and father who are getting on in years. I don't have much else to do with my money.

I stayed with the show for another couple of weeks before abandoning it outside of Denver. I was going to hang around in Denver for a few days before hopping a freight to San Francisco. I wanted to get a ship to Hawaii. After that, I'd probably head back to New York City.

I did.

Rather than having a wife and kid and respectable job in a well-off neighbourhood, the brother was a nasty piece of work, a scabrous junkie who shared a room on Avenue C with several other mean, scabrous junkies. His goal in life was to open his own meth lab. Meanwhile, he broke into cars, climbed up fire escape ladders and got into apartments, and turned tricks to get what he needed to score. He called his brother a freak and an embarrassment. "My brother is the fucking Alligator Man in the fucking circus, man," he announced to the others lying around on piss-stained mattresses.

"Right?" he asked me, to validate his claim.

"It's the carnival, not the circus," I told him.

As I was leaving, he said he'd blow me for fifteen bucks.

I had friends with a big, old fashioned six room apartment on the Lower East Side, at Grand and Bowery. They told me I could stay there and I wound up being based there for nearly three years when I migrated to Canada.

My first New York job was in a magazine warehouse uptown. There were magazines dating back to the turn of the century and beyond, and people all over North America were eager to get hold of the, I'd be handed a stack of orders and hustle up and down the stairs to fill them. I was big on Henry Miller in those days and had an early bibliography of his work. One of his earliest publications was in a little review called *Jazzis*, and they actually had it, as well as much of the rest of his stuff from the late teens and early Twenties. That stuff was worth a lot of money then and worth a fortune

Other than the boss of the warehouse, I was the only white employee

There were American born blacks, Puerto Rican blacks and Jamaicans and they strongly disliked each other. The American blacks had a distinctly American attitude. They hated everybody. I had a Puerto Rican friend named Joey. We'd pal around and he'd get hassled for doing so by a local black guy named Arthur. I tried to ignore Arthur but Joey would talk back to him. He'd look at me or Joey and nod knowingly. Once he said, "Just wait."

My employment ended after I'd been at the warehouse for a month. The boss called me into the office and told me he was going to have to let me go.

"Why?" I asked. "I like it here and I think I do a decent job."

"I like having you here and you do a fine job. But Arthur accused you of calling him a nigger."

"I never did that."

"I believe you but he's threatened to report me to the ACLU and the NAACP unless I fire you. He says otherwise he's going to get a lawyer."

"That's blackmail, Mort."

"Yeah, but what can I do? I don't need the hassle. The place will be surrounded by pickets. I'm afraid I have to let you go."

Mort handed me a pay envelope, "There's a little bonus in there and I'll supply a good reference."

And, so, I was free to go job hunting.

It only took me an hour or two to get another job. This at an Italian grocery store on Avenue C. One of the reasons I was hired on the spot was because I knew the Italian meats and cheeses. And I could tell escarole from Boston Lettuce. You want the choicest eggplant for your polenta, I'll choose one.

I'd be sent out on deliveries carrying a paper bag or two of groceries. Most of the deliveries were to a couple of high-rise apartment buildings in the neighbourhood. There was so much crime in the area and so much fear of crime that these deliveries were a time-consuming procedure.

For instance, I'd ring the apartment number on the board in the vestibule, wait for a voice on the intercom; After telling them I was from Fabrizzio's grocery, I'd be told to wait there until somebody could come down. Grocery delivery days were always arranged in advance. Most of the customers were elderly and they would have a son or grandson to visit and oversee the procedure. So, the son would come down to the lobby and check me out. If he was not afraid, he'd buzz me in, not into the main lobby but to a sort of antechamber. I'd show the bag and the order slip then I'd usually but not always be let in. It sometimes took me an entire eight-hour shift to make four deliveries.

I got along fine with the boss. I liked working at the store but I had the itch to travel so I'd leave New York and come back to it time after time. I went to West Chester, and worked as a census taker and when I was done, worked in a laundry outlet just off campus.

I was hired by the L.H. Percy Company in Philadelphia to sell space in a year book whose purpose was to raise money for volunteer firemen. This was like a license to print money, small money. Most businesses were only too eager to pay for space in the book. The logic behind the project was that businesses would be happy to be presented in the yearbook. They'd be buying an ad while simultaneously taking pride in doing a good deed.

The firemen got a third of the revenue, me a third and Percy forty percent.

The office was in a row house in the beautiful old part of Philadelphia, one of those big houses had been there since the early seventeen hundreds. I could almost imagine wily old Ben Franklin strolling along Walnut Street heading for his printing press.

After that yearbook, I was invited to do the same work for a similar book for an architects' society. The rates were higher and therefore I'd make more money for each sale but sales would be more difficult because the community service angle was missing. But the main drawback, the one that made me resign was that Mr. Percy insisted I cut my hair very short and dress conservatively.

Around this time, I missed out on another job for the same reasons. I answered an ad in the *Philadelphia Bulletin* announcing that the Coatesville Record was seeking a sports reporter.

Coatesville is a small city forty miles from Philadelphia and ten miles from West Chester, my old stomping grounds. I didn't figure I had much of a chance because the record was a daily paper and usually to work on a daily, a prospective reporter was required to have put in time on a weekly paper. I applied nevertheless, and was told to write a fictitious account of a college football game. I did, and not only was I accepted, they offered me the job of sports editor.

The salary would be good and the work undemanding but the job came with the proviso that I straighten up what he called 'my act'. Unlike L.H. Percy the Managing Editor elucidated, "You dress somewhat like a cross between a mafia capo and a street corner nigger. You'll need to get along with players and coaches and you can't do it the way you look"

I didn't need to be sports editor that badly.

Next, got a job with an exterminator company. I was to learn the business and begin my rise to the top of the rat and cockroach killing world.

I went out that first and only day with an Italian guy in his thirties named Ignacio. People called the office in Northeast Philadelphia to complain about rats and bugs. So we sallied fort with a list of these callers. I toted a pack with a spray can and various powders in metal containers.

That job lasted half a day. The first stop was simple and straight forward. We left lines of white powdery poison along likely rat routes. The second stop was at a small place occupied by a black woman and her two children. She carried her little girl cradled in her arms. She asked Ignace whether the powder would be harmful to her babies.

"Oh, no!" replied Ignace, "Not at all."

So saying, he grabbed a piece of sliced white bread from the table and put some of the powder on it. He proceeded to take a bite of the bread then handed it to the little girl. I grabbed it out of her hand and she looked at me in shock and started to cry. The mother gave me a ferocious look.

"Madame," I said "This is highly poisonous and liable to kill a child."

I'd seen that there was no rat poison on the corner of the slice of bread that Ignace had eaten.

I stood up and walked out of there, followed but a very angry Ignacio. Down on the street he shouted at me for losing us a sale.

"I saw what you did. That kid would have died."

"So? what's another dead nigger!"

After that I went back to the carnival and a better class of people.

Somewhere in Missouri I got hooked up with the Magnificent Ambrose, an old-time Psychic. He would tell strangers in the audience about their present and their past. He did this by considering what he observed, by basic psychology and, most importantly, by research. I came along at the perfect time; he had just fired his latest assistant. As his helper I did the research which consisted of circulating among the audience and eaves dropping. I either conveyed the information to him in person or by a complex system of verbal codes."

"Harry" (his real name, "The old biddy in the third seat from the left in the second row caught her husband fooling around in the barn with the neighbour's daughter. She knew he was fooling around with something but was afraid it was the little heifer, and she told her friend the harridan siting next to her, 'I don't want none of them cow diseases.'"

I won't reveal how the codes worked.

I went back to New York and put in a month or so working on the docks, getting hired at shape ups by Penn Industries on the Hudson, Then, I got a pleasant job at the public library in West Chester where I stocked shelves and helped customers as much as I was able. I found an apartment across the street and went between it and the one in New York. They were good to me in the library and although I resigned after four months they hired me back the next year to do much more interesting chores. I went out on the book mobile with a creep who told the library director that I scared the patrons. He was always going on about Commies and their dupes and how people like me should be put in camps. He badmouthed me to the Director and she'd roll her eyes when telling me the story.

Soon I was driving the bookmobile myself, not to outposts where borrowers awaited but at night to show films at other libraries in the county system. This was great fun, especially when I met a former carnival sword swallower named Daniel P. Mannix. He was also a naturalist and a tracker of unusual animals. He had made a documentary about the creatures of Central America which was very popular at the screenings. After meeting him and heading his book, *Memoirs of a Sword Swallower*, I came up with idea of his accompanying me in the book mobile and giving a talk after I showed his film. This proved to be extremely popular.

It was great associating with Mannix. At first, after I told him, I had a bit of carnival experience, he'd test me. I happened go mention that I knew Lamond Stovall, the alligator man. Well, if I knew the Alligator man I must be a decent fellow. When he learned I also had met Francis O'Connor, I was even invited out to the old family home on the Main Line, where houses date back to colonial times. The Mannix place had a couple of acres and the grounds eae occupied by capabaras and anteaters and other creatures not usually seen in those parts. He'd have luncheons or dinner parties where the guests would be extra fat ladies, guides he'd known in Central America and Admirals in the Navy.

I have little concept of the chronology of all these jobs and travel. I do know that sometime during 1966, I put in a couple of months as an apprentice meat cutter at a butcher shop in Havertown,

Pennsylvania. I started by putting together packs of ground meat. The ground beef had some beef in it but it was equal parts trimmed beef fat and fat from other hunks of meat, pork mostly. It also consisted of the oily waste I scraped from the innards of the electric saws. The saws were mounted on stands and doors provided access to the insides should a belt needed to be replaced or repairs made. These compartments also revealed the bottoms of the saw blades. The blades and the motors had to be oiled, the fat collected at the blade housing. This gelatinous mess was gathered by the assistant meat cutter and added to the small amount of meat and the large amount of fat gathered from above.

Trucks filled with sides of beef backed up in the alley and the driver muscled in the meat, usually entire quarter sections. He'd struggled with the quarters but the hoofs were tied together with wire. He had to push this over to an overhead roller system where I waited holding the hook, with curled thumb and index finger, and aim to get the wire of the tied hoofs over the hook. It was dangerous for both of us. He could damage his back, and I could crush my fingers.

I boned a lot of chickens at my block. I got so I could do it with my eyes closed. But I was so enthused about going to Hawaii that my fingers collected quite a few cuts, whether my eyes were open or closed.

In San Francisco I got on a ship going to Honolulu. The deal was I'd work my way over and get a free return trip.

I looked up an old high school friend in Honolulu and she showed me the elephant. The mass tourist boom was just getting started, big hotels seemed to be sprouting from the sands. One day we went over to Molokai where the leper colony had been, where Father Damien had come from Belgium to tend to the lepers knowing full well that he'd contract the disease.

I nearly decided to stay in Hawaii but I was a restless fool, and reluctantly caught my ship back to the mainland.

In those days I would frequently wind up in the carnival, just as later landscaping would keep me going.

I was working for Cosmos Attractions, named for the bossman George Cosmopolous. I started out in another lowly job, ride boy, operating the merry go round. It's in the carnival that I became a temporary capitalist. I had some money saved and bought half of the merry go round from Arvin, the mechanic. He could fix anything which was great because the merry go round needed plenty of fixing.

The show's big earner Was Billy Bondari who besides having some mysterious and unspecified aging disease, was possessed of a tail. Probably no more than sixteen or seventeen he looked like a particularly weathered sixty.

His tail bone was a foot and a half in length, dipped down then up and swooped back down like the first part f a roller coaster track. Billy's tail was rigid and obviously caused him logistic problems as well as constant pain. It hurt every time he bumped against something. He had an optimistic attitude that astounded me given his condition.

"Thank God for the carnie," he'd say in his deep old man's voice, sometimes adding, "And Dunny and Donna."

This was an elderly couple who looked after him They weren't related and no one seemed to know how they'd gotten together. It was obvious though that they loved this unusual little person.

One person who didn't love him or, it seemed, anyone else in the show was a man called Emmet Toohey.

He was the manager of the ten-on-one, the sideshow.

Toohey criticized and made fun of everybody. There was a hermaphrodite in the show called Johnnie, and Emmett took great pleasure in badmouthing her, "Well what the hell are you, man or woman?"

He called me a stupid juvenile delinquent and Billy an animal that ought to be hanging from a tree branch. Most everyone ignored his insults; they were used to them but Moxie the five hundred pound lady would trade with him.

"   Moxie, you're a disgrace. Guy needs a thirty-six inch dick to screw you."

"You're right and that's thirty-five inches more than you got. Johnnie has a bigger one than you."

Tensions increased on the lot. Emmett was out of hand and I

heard someone talk about taking a pipe wrench to him. I considered it to be talk until the afternoon Emmett made fun of Billy which was not unusual but this time Billy began to cry. Emmett laughed at him and committed the unpardonable sin of pulling Billy's tail.

I expected the carnies to jump on Emmett right away and tear him apart but they just backed away.

We went about the business of running the show as usual. After the tear down there seemed to be a strange electricity going around. I knew something was up. Unk Howard, an old-time showman and sort of a beloved uncle figure around the show—hence his nickname—told me to follow him to his trailer where we'd have a nip or two and cut up touches. Whenever I tried to bring the subject around to Emmett and his dastardly behaviour, Unk diverted me with another great story.

I've been very fortunate in my life to have associated with, and listened to, some of the greatest story tellers: carnies, old boxing people and hoboes.

Unk Howard and Marcel Horne, Marty Cohen and Nick Zubray, Floyd Wallace and Lord Open Road (James H. Langford) their like have gone forever and will never come again. The world is a poorer place. Now you can take a story telling course.

That night Unk told me if I was ever in Truckee I should look up his old friend Frances Marie, who spent her life as a railroad man. When he was done, Unk looked at his watch and began telling me of an old carnie acrobat who used to get on top of Pullman cars and walk along the boards on his hands. This on a moving train. A seemingly impossible feat.

Around about midnight there was a knock on the trailer door. He opened it. Someone spoke to him and then Unk told me to come with him.

At the end of the midway sat the merry go round. A pole light was shining down on a pickup truck and into a hole in the ground. We reached the site and Arvin handed me a shovel. I looked down into where everyone else was looking. It was Emmett Toohey down there in the hole.

It's your turn, you're a carnie, one of use, and we're all in this together. Three or four shovels full, and pass it along."

The carnivals provided a temporary escape from
The social conditions of the outise or 'normal' world.

The War sickened me; the racial situation sickened me.
In other words, the United States itself sickened me.

I mailed my draft card back to them, the authorities. They returned it.

I was 1-A so I enrolled at a black college notoriously easy to get into, Cheyney State. I was one of only five white students. I didn't have any trouble there but I kept going up to New York City which didn't help my grades. I knew I would go to Canada so I didn't worry over much about grades.

I was summoned for preinduction but didn't show up. I was working at the Italian grocery on the Lower East Side then and I was pleased to be doing so. Who had time to play that game when I knew the final outcome.

It came about soon enough. I was summoned to be inducted along with a hundred and fifty other males my age.

There at the Armory on Broad Street in Philadelphia we were ordered to take all our clothes off and toe a line painted across the floor. After the bulldog sergeant barked out his speech about honour and patriotism, we were told to step forward 'and be inducted into the American military. I didn't think I'd be the only one not to take that step but I was. This occasioned some loud and harsh words and provoked many of the others to turn and look at me. I could see from the expressions on the faces of many of them that they, too, wanted no part of the whole deal. Others were plain scared. The majority of the young men were black, and I couldn't fathom why they'd want to risk their lives for a country that treated them the way it did and always had done.

The sergeant again ordered me to step forward and I refused.

"That's an order, god dam it."

"I'm not in the Army and I don't have to do what you say."

"You'll do what I say when I get you in the backroom."

I had to walk naked down the line – part of the continued humiliation—to the small holding room. There was a black guy in drag in there, looking dejected.

The Sargant came in and told him. "Take off your dress, sweetie and join the others."

When he'd gone, the flattop fool, said, "If he can't get away with that, you think I'm going to let you get away with being a fucking conscientious objector?"

I put in a call to a lawyer. I'd been carrying his number around for year. He was connected. The problem was 'Those People" were patriots but the lawyer had other people to answer to and I walked out of there.

Out of there and into my car and came to Canada. I had all the necessary immigration papers and a written promise of a job. I had been to Ottawa, and a Carleton University professor put in a word for me at a department store in the old Bytown section of the city.

I went back to New York and West Chester to get my stuff and headed to Canada to stay. Two days after crossing the border I was working on a delivery truck for Slover's Department store. I was hired as a swamper, a truck driver's helper and the driver was a French Canadian fellow. I had never met a French Canadian fellow before.

He knew my situation was tenuous and took advantage of it to make me do most of the work.

At one point I got a fridge we were delivering onto a dolly and was struggling to push it across the lawn to a house. "Hey, excuse me, Jean Pierre but I could use a little help getting this three hundred-pound fridge to the door."

He didn't appreciate my entreaty.

After a few weeks, I was called into the director's office and told I was being transferred to a branch store and given a job selling men's clothing. He regarded this as a reward for good service. When I expressed my reluctance he said, "Look at it this way you won't have to work with a frog."

He allowed as how I didn't have a choice. I was a temporary landed immigrant and my conduct would be monitored for a year. In other words quitting wasn't a good idea.

So, I sold men's clothes. Ironically the one other salesman was French Canadian.

It was the middle of October when I started at the main store downtown, and now Christmas was coming up. I didn't have any family ties in Ottawa or anywhere in Canada so, when asked, I agreed to work through the holidays. They promised me time and a half and a bonus.

When the first week of January came around and I got my paycheck, I saw it included neither time and a half nor the bonus. When I pointed this out to the manager, he told me in so many words, "So what?

What are you going to do about it?"

I decided to tell him and to hell with any harm to my status. I quit and immediately got a six week 'casual' job at the Department of Labour library. It was a good job and I liked it. Had they offered to take me on permanently I might have taken it. My chores weren't demanding and I made a friend with whom I would be friends until he died fifty years later. That was Vernon Mackelvie, the assistant director and a true eccentric who denied being an eccentric, a true sign. He had an egg-shaped head and pear-shaped body which he covered in hand tailored s. He even got his shoes custom made by an elderly cobbler. Vernon liked old books and old movies so we had a lot in common right there. Only one person at the library didn't care for him and that, unfortunately was the Director. That must have been the reason the Director didn't care for me, either. At first, I thought it might be because I was an American but then I noticed the way he would look at Vernon. Added to that was the fact that the women doted on Vernon and were stand offish with him.

One morning as I was pushing my tray along the cafeteria line at lunch time, the man at my side engaged me in conversation. He was sharply pressed with combed back black hair. The lady cashier deferred to him and called him by name which meant nothing to me. We ate lunch together after which he suggested me go to the Chateau Laurier for a drink. I demurred saying I only had a hour break plus I was new at the job and didn't want to screw things up. He told me to trust him and not worry about it.

I knew he wasn't a homosexual so I went along.

People greeted him like he was an important guy and I began to wonder who he was. After a couple drinks, he said, "Now, I'm okay to face those bastards."

I followed him outside and we walked to the Parliament buildings There," he said, "Look, I have to go inside for a cabinet meeting. I wish I could bring you in to take notes or something but they wouldn't allow it. Why don't you get another drink and meet me in an hour and a half."

Well, I thought, what the hell, I can always find another job but I had coffee instead and read the paper.

When he finally emerged, we walked back to the Department of Labour building. "They're going to fire me," I said.

"No, they're not," my new friend replied.

When the elevator reached the library floor, the man held the door open. The Director came striding over asking me who I thought I was butt hen he saw who I was with he abruptly shut up.

Suddenly, it was all bowing and scraping, and Y'es Minster."

"Now, listen up," the fellow said, his speech a little slurred. My friend Jimmy's been helping me out. I hope none of you give him a hard time."

He looked squarely at the Director then wrote something on the back of a business card, and handed it to me. "My home number. Any trouble, give me a call."

I noticed Vernon in the background with a very pleased smile on his face.

The man and I Shook hands. "See you, Jimmy."

"Later, Bryce."

The Director immediately started hassling me as the elevator rose up.

I looked at the front of the card. The man was Bryce Mackasey, the minister of Labour.

"None of that," I told the Director. You heard the man, If you have a problem phone the Minister. I'm sure he'll appreciate you phoning him at home."

My job was to catalogue the papers, reports and pamphlets that came in every day. Other than that, I took care of any visitor that showed up, directed them to a table and made sure they had whatever books or papers they wanted. Other than that, I didn't have much to do so I prowled the stacks, looking at production comparisons between Canadian steel mills in the 1930s and those of Eastern Europe. It was in those shelves that I first heard of and read about Stakhanovism.

When my stint at the library came to an end, I applied for work at the Salvation Army thrift store in Ottawa. The guy told me his son was studying Journalism at Carleton and he sure hoped that when the kid was 23, he wouldn't be so low down as to have to apply to the Salvation Army for a job. I thanked him very much and went across to Crawley Films. I'd had an eight millimeter camera for a couple of years and went around filming what ever struck my fancy. I knew Crawley Films made interesting documentaries, and the head Budge Crawley had a good reputation. It seemed a natural.

There was a young guy in there, my sage or a couple of years older who listened to me and summoned the boss.

I told Budge Crawley that I'd take whatever work he hade available, even if it wasn't film work. I'd even sweep the floors. He laughed at me. "I guess you think you'll make big feature films one day and it'll make a great story, how you started sweeping the floor, paying your dues until you won your Oscar. Eh? You're so naïve."

"No, sir. I just want a job."

He was still laughing as I walked out of there.

Fifty years later, I made contact with a woman named Jenny Scolding, author of a memoir *Vagabond Girl*. She informed me that she had a flat across the street from the Sally Anne at that exact time, and the young guy in the Crawley office might have been her boyfriend, who was a son of Budge Crawley.

I had taken a photography course at the Ottawa YMCA, and learned basic composition and how to develop and print. I therefore felt confident to answer an ad in the Citizen for a new magazine that wanted a photographer.

The magazine was called *North Country Living* and the first issue was to appear in two months.

It was run out of a small office by a middle-aged man and woman, obviously a couple.

They hired me on the spot which should have made me suspicious.

"Your first assignment will be to take some good shots of cows."

"Where do I find cows around here?"

"In the Ottawa Valley. I'll give you directions. But that won't take long. In the meantime, before the book comes out, you can earn some money by selling ads. We'll pay you a thirty percent commission."

He gave me a rate sheet and I hit the bricks. I did all right, too; people were friendly and the prospectus was appealing. There were recommendations from people I never heard of but who had important jobs, President of this and Director of that. One of the blurbs was supplied by someone even I had heard of, Pierre Trudeau.

I walked the streets, calling at shops, getting to know the downtown. After a week, I figured I was owed about two hundred dollars but when I went on the appointed Friday to collect my earnings, the woman told me there had been a slight problem setting up their new business account. She assured me things would be set right any day now.

I took a day off to go out to the Ottawa Valley and got what I thought were some decent shots of cows. They cooperated with the novice by approaching the fence, standing still and staring.

That done I went back to hustling ads. I was in a sporting goods store on Banks Street giving my story to the young clerk and showing him the fancy brochure,

"Looks good," he said. "I'll get the boss from the back". While he was finding his boss, an announcement came of the radio warning merchants to beware of a salesman purporting to represent a magazine called *North Country Living*. "The salesman is in his Twenties and has a distinct American accent. There is no such magazine."

I immediately took my leave. I hurried to the office where the lights were off and the woman was frantically packing up. The cops had been phoning and people knocking on the door. She muttered some excuses and something about a big misunderstanding.

"Look, I don't care about that. So, it was a put-up job. Just give me the money you owe me. Four hundred bucks by now."

"I'll give you what I have."

She fumbled some bills out of her handbag. I picked them up from the desk while she told me I better hide out, "or split town."

And that's how I got to be a Toronto resident. I figured cops would be patrolling the bus and train stations. I had a friend take me an hour out of the city where I caught a bus, alighting at the station on Dundas Street in Toronto.

I got a room for the night at the lowly Ford Hotel, notorious for being the hideout of James Earle Ray.

My first job in the area was at a warehouse in Etobicoke. It lasted an entire three hours or until lunch time. The owner sat across from me at the lunch and remarked on my accent. He asked me if I was a draft dodger, and I told him that I was. He told me he didn't want any 'pinko draft dodgers'—his actual words—working at his place.

Next, I got a job in a factory on the line wrapping porcelain figurines with papers and putting them in little white boxes. There were people who'd been standing over the conveyor belt for years doing the same job, making the exact same little moves a thousand times a day. No one would speak for fear of being distracted and messing up the flow.

I drove a delivery van filled with lighting fixtures and put in some time at an electronics warehouse.

I responded to a want ad in the Toronto Star and applied for a truck driver's job at Simpson Sears. The personnel manager told me they had filled that position but would I be interested in a job in the catalogue layout department. I said Sure and the next day was preparing copy and fitting words and images into the available catalogue spaces. It wasn't exactly copywriting because you had chunks of words to choose from, like 'assorted colours" and "up to date styling."

It wasn't exactly arduous and I stayed with it for six months. Simpson Sears was in an interesting part of Toronto and I worked with some good people. The office was close to Massey Hall and some great watering holes like the Brass Rail. There's a classic jazz album featuring Charlie Parker, Charlie Mingus, Dizzy Gillespie, Bud Powell and Max Roach live at Massey Hall. The night of the concert coincided with the Jersey Jo Walcott-Rocky Marciano heavyweight championship bout. The musicians kept cutting out and running down to the Brass Rail to catch some of the action on the television screens.

There was a different kind of action on Mutual Street in the day time, too courtesy of a guy who sold his privately printed poems on the south side of the street and another guy on north side who sat on the curb every day and masturbated. Regulars ignored him.

Another man dressed in white robes and had wires connecting himself to a metal pole, to "dispel negative energy" he said.

At work I became friends with Dave 'Farley'. He'd had polio as a youth and it was painful to watch him walk dragging his leg. He didn't mind a drink or two after work and I often kept him company. It wasn't just this fondness for beer and Bushmills that landed him in Toronto from his prairie city. Dave loved country music and had been the all-night disc jockey at a country radio station. There was a notorious local woman who wasn't a stranger to alcohol herself and at night she'd go around to whatever businesses that might be open and offer sexual favours for a bottle or a few of bucks to buy one.

Well, Dave who had trouble finding dates, succumbed to the woman's entreaties. Their rendezvous occurred in the recording booth and Dave discovered when they were done that he had left the microphone on.

He was fired before his shift ended. The station owner came down, kicked him out and finished the shift himself. For awhile the incident was the talk of the town but Dave was long gone before people had stopped talking about it.

The French copy department was on the same floor as the English. I fell in with one of the French copy writers, and one day over coffee, he pointed at my paperback copy of poems by Blaise Cendrars. "You know, Cendrars gave me what must have been the last interview of his life. It was for my school paper in Paris. I had written him a letter never dreaming he would answer let along agree to see me. When his wife replied to my letter I felt intimidated. I went to see him and he was confined to bed. He couldn't even hold a pen in his hand. It was sad but he was very friendly though I could hardly understand what he said. I was practically in tears when I left his house."

There was a meeting of copy and layout departments in the different branches. At that get together I became friendly with a fellow from the suburban branch. He was my age and we discovered we had some things in common. Not only were we both draft dodgers, we'd both spent time researching and investigating the Kennedy assassination. In Philadelphia, I had done some minor work for Vincent Salandria, a lawyer and former school teacher from South Philadelphia who was sort of a stringer for James Garrison, the New Orleans District Attorney who was involved in unravelling threads of the conspiracy.

Joe Nickell resigned from Simpson Sears and eventually I did too. Joe was also a magician and soon became magician in residence at the Houdini Museum in Niagara Falls. He went on to have many other personas, declaring, "I've made a profession out of professions."

He was a croupier and a river boat guide before eventually getting into forensics. For years now he has been the world's only full-time, paid investigator of the paranormal.

After I quit Simpson-Sears I went to Europe, and came back resolved to get involved in radical politics, an activity that was neglected when I came north. I had come to the conclusion that protests and demonstrations were as futile as working within the system. They mainly served to supply content for the television news. I decided to start an underground newspaper. My girl friend said she knew a printer. I met the fellow. He said he merely operated an offset machine but he lived in a Co-op house on Bathurst Street, and he and his mates were "talking about doing something."

When I asked him, like what? He replied, like starting a record co-op. I replied that there were plenty of outlets for buying records but only one alternative newspaper and that was an ugly, ill-written and sloppily produced hippy rag.

It took me all winter to convince them a newspaper was a good idea. They were mostly student power types from the University of Windsor, and addicted to meetings. These people had the sort of communist leanings gleaned from union activity at the auto plants. The kind of ideas that would make Wobblies weep.

When I said we had to find an artist they were astounded by the notion. Someone had a sister who knew a graphic artist and he came to a meeting. He and I got along, the two outsiders. When the meetings lasted into the Spring, I said, "Look, this paper will never get done unless we do it ourselves. So, Robert Macdonald designed it and I wrote most of it and from the moment it came off the presses it was a success.

I hadn't put any money into the paper so I made a deal to hustle advertising and sell the paper on the street. I hawked the paper on street corners for 25 cents. When I sold twenty-five papers I gave all the money to the office and then kept ten cents for every subsequent paper. Things were cheap in Toronto in those days. I could get a roast beef or ham and cheese sandwich at the corner store for forty-cents. I wrote an article about a great Chinese restaurant called the Peter Pan, and the owner stood me to a couple of free dinners.

At the same time, I began to manage a 'progressive' rock band called Boogie Dick. We'd go to gigs in suburban halls and barely make gas money. Our only success was when I booked them into the Paramount Tavern on Spadina Avenue, This was a tougher, real deal version of Grossman's Tavern two blocks up the street that hippie types considered to be a 'People's' bar.

The winter of that year, 1970-'71 I somehow got to be the Super of a duplex on Howland Avenue. I lived at #54 and would later be super at 56. The duplex was owned by two brothers named Greenbaum. Their uncle had been a CBC announcer but went to Hollywood and became a star under the name Lorne Green.

In exchange for a free room, I collected rents and did minor repairs. The brothers never got big repairs done.

I was getting by okay, what with no rent to pay and the occasional cheque from the *Globe and Mail* for a book review.

Things always needed doing at the house, and to do them I had to buy parts usually from Weiner's hardware down on Bloor Street. The brothers were reluctant to pay for these so I felt no compunction in having one of the hardware guys give me an inflated receipt that I would try to collect on.

One day a bedraggled dark-skinned couple knocked on the front door, clad in sweaters against the February cold. They had come to Toronto from El Salvador, walking a good part of the way. Someone somewhere had given them my name and once in Toronto were able to get my address from some social service agency.

I fixed them up with a room, the attic room which was too cold to rent out. I managed to get a space heater from somewhere and they were embarrassingly grateful.

It was a great time and even the annoying things could be dealt with or laughed off. My younger brother Dave showed up from the States. He had no money so I let him sleep in an unused room in the back that held all manner of junk. I remember a fifty-pound burlap bag of chestnuts which was there the entire year I was at 54 and the whole year I spent next door at 56.

I rented a room to a red-headed Christian Scientist hooker named Denise. I'd see her on Bloor Street at the lowdown Metropolitan Café soliciting customers. Back to 54 she would drag the sorriest customers. She indefatigable, forever knocking on the door or stepping into the shower with you. The bathroom door didn't lock.

"Hey, no charge!" she'd say.

One tenant who didn't offer her favours for free was a curvaceous young woman, second floor rear, who wanted to make an exchange for rent. She was cute and always – always – dressed in black leather. He boyfriend was a biker without a bike. He didn't seem to care what she did. I never succumbed.

A Trinidadian woman on the second floor had a foot tall, hard rubber statue of Colonel Sanders on her dresser. She'd call me often to do a little chore for her. One afternoon, I glanced at Colonel Sanders and at her and raised my eyebrows. She sputtered forth a fusillade of giggles.

I rented a room to a fellow we called John the Baptist. He dressed in a long brown woolen cape with a hood to protect his shaved head. He was forever preaching, and people were forever telling him to shut up.

I kept rent money in a metal Band aid tin in a drawer of my heavy wooden desk. One thing that did annoy me was that my brother got into the habit of pilfering a few bucks every week when he knew there was something in the box. I told him to stop but he didn't. So, this made me hustle more vigorously to make up the difference. The Weiner Brothers were most cooperative.

There was a quiet woman across the hall from me, in the other front room. I thought she was single but it turned out she was married to a tall handsome black-haired fellow who came by every few days to see her. He was a Romany, a gypsy, and his people had forbidden him to marry his gaudja girl friend. When they learned he had defied them, he was not permitted to bring her around. He was as quiet as she was, reserved like most gypsy men, at least until you got close.

He took to hanging around and keeping an eye on the place. It was surprising given the variety of street life that there wasn't much crime. He started his vigilance after telling me he caught a guy sneaking into my room and coming out with bills in his hand. I told him that was my brother but he didn't believe me because 'brothers wouldn't do that sort of thing.'

The landlords were suspicious of the Romany boyfriend.

"What the nationality is that guy?" they asked me.

I told them and one of the brothers said, "We can't have any gypsies around here."

"People say the same things about Jews."

"But we don't steal like gypsies. They'll rob you blind."

"I was only kidding," I countered. "He's Portuguese."

There was another roomer whom the brothers didn't like, Danny Pearlmutter. They called him Daniel if they had to speak to him. He was a co-religionist but unsuccessful in their estimation, being a bohemian living on welfare.

He was my age with a curly mop of black hair and the beginnings of a beard. He didn't look like he'd ever done a lick of work in his life but he was obsessed with work songs.

He talked about black railroad and plantation songs, and chain gang songs and sea chanteys, how the lead man would chant and the other men come in on a chorus of grunts or exhalations

But he traced these words songs back to the ancient Greeks who had songs for all kinds of work. He said there was even a whole range of fountain songs, sung through the ages by women hauling water.

This led to hawkers songs which I'd heard throughout childhood. The knife grinder, the vegetable dealer, the flower seller, they each had their cry or call.

As if there weren't enough strange people living in the building, the street outside could have been peopled by characters from Balzac or Dostoevski.

There was a Jamaican called Stiff Kenny who so ramrod straight, walked slanted backwards. He never said a word. Another Jamaican guy, an ugly, twisted, little fellow who always had a story to tell about the latest woman he had gotten pregnant. To hear him tell it, he'd fathered hundreds of children with hundreds of women.

And then there was the Shuffler. This poor fellow was out there every day not really walking but shuffling. He moved by little half steps, never lifting a foot off the pavement.

Once when I talked to him, he told me all about his round trip from Fredericton to Toronto when he was a young man. "But, Shuffler,"

I said, "This is Toronto."

"What!"

"You're in Toronto now, not Fredericton."

He looked at me with his sad eyes, "Don't kid an old man, son."

One day I saw him on Howland Avenue making his way the half block down to Bloor Street. I had to go down to King and Front Streets so I cut over to the Bathurst subway station and started my journey. I went to my destination, did my business, loitered in a coffee shop and retraced my steps. When I got back to Howland Avenue the Shuffler had just reached Bloor Street.

Then there was Ace Miller, known as the world's oldest thief. When I first encountered him, he had just gotten out of the joint after serving a couple of weeks for shoplifting.

His specialty was overcoats; in fact, he was obsessed by overcoats. You'd see him wearing a brand new coat and carrying one over each arm. How he got them out of Eaton's I had no idea.

So, everyone was making a little money somehow. The Jamaican lover claimed his many women gave him money. Ace stole coats. I had my petty hustles and wrote my book reviews but it wasn't enough. Oh, I fed and clothed myself but I needed money for trips so I started hanging out at Queen and Sherbourne Streets, southeast corner, where in the morning there was a sort of shape-up. You stood around and people needing help would drive up and make a choice. I was young and strong looking so I usually got picked. The first time I did it I moved refrigerators all day. From a boxcar to the man's truck, after which we drove them to different stores. When the truck was empty. we went back to the boxcar for another load.

There was an employment agency near the intersection, a few doors west of Sherbourne. Occasionally they sent me out on job. The advantage of this was that the employer had to pay you whereas some of the people who hired you from the intersection, tried to stiff you for the money and you usually didn't have any way to get hold of them.

The disadvantage of the agency was that you had to be there at six in the morning to have a good chance of getting hired. What I got hired for that first time was helping a fellow put up gyprock. By 'helping' I mean I muscled the sheets into place and lugged around his supplies. That lasted for a five-day work week and after I was done one day, I went for an early dinner and made a friend.

You do these jobs and meet plenty of people but not many of these relationships continue beyond work hours. This fellow had and unruly mop of red hair and a thick down east accent. We had previously encountered each other at the intersection and that very morning at the agency.

He was as enthusiastic as a kid and with that hair he resembled one. Like a thousand other guys, he had come to Toronto from the Maritimes in search of work.

"There was nothing for me back there anymore," he said.

I ran into him a couple more times before we got on a job together. This was at a soft drink plant washing bottles. The work lasted three or hour days. One afternoon when work was over, we went for a beer in the Dominion House at Queen and Sumach. At one point he looked around the pub at the other drinkers and asked me, "You ever wonder when you're in a place like this what all these other people do?"

"Sure," I said. And I wonder where they live. I mean what kinds of places."

"Really? You think like that?"

"Sure."

"I never met anybody else who thinks those kinds of things."

He had a girl friend who was also from Newfoundland. He hadn't known her back home, but they were drawn together by nostalgia.

His girl friend had a friend, and I was introduced to her. The four of us went out together a couple times, but there wasn't any spark between the girl and I.

Due to the vagaries of our work lives, a couple of weeks went by when I didn't see my new pal. When I finally caught up with him, he looked tired and unhappy.

"You two split up?" I asked.

He nodded, "Yeah, she went back home."

"Are you going after her?"

"No, it's over and like I said, there's nothing else for me there."

One morning a week or so later, I went to see him in his room above the Derby Tavern. The smell of last night's draught beer seeped up through the floor boards, and the view out the window was as bleak as his mood. There was the dishwater sky and the backs of dreary warehouses. Across the street was the streetcar turn around and old people huddled in overcoats waited for the car.

There was no lifting him out of his mood, so after an hour or so, I left.

Another couple of weeks passed and when I ran into him his mood had completely changed. He was smiling and ebullient.

"Alberta," he said. "That's the place. There's plenty of work in Alberta. Like on oil rigs. In a few weeks, come Spring I'm going to head out there."

"Sounds like a good idea."

"Sure is, why don't you go out with me?"

I had nothing going on. I was only hanging around waiting to hear the lion roar while I lay in bed. I mean this quite literally. The old Toronto Zoo was in the Don Valley ravine and if you lived at the east end of Carlton

Or Wellesley Street you could hear the lion roar at night. I thought it would be great to have a room in the neighbourhood and be in bed with a girl one when the old lion let loose.

Over weeks, I had been checking out the houses over looking the Valley but there no rooms for rent. Finally, a guy I knew asked me if I would room stay in his room for a couple of weeks to keep it safe while he was in London.

So, I eagerly took up residence. And I did hear the old lion roar at night but, alas, I didn't have a girl friend.

My friend and I got jobs unloading boxcars down by the Don River but I worked the early shift and he came on in the afternoon. One day we made plans to meet up at night for beer and conversation at the Gerrard House. My pal liked the bouncer there. A short, wide old-fashioned looking Scotsman who had, apparently, never been beaten by any of those who challenged him. There were plenty of these because of his reputation.

Anyway, I got to the Gerrard House but my pal who was usually early hadn't show up. I waited for an hour and a half and left I figured he had met a woman and was off having fun, or maybe not.

The next day, I got to the job and the foreman said, "Too bad about your buddy."

"What? What do you mean?"

"You haven't heard? He was killed yesterday afternoon when one of the boxcars wasn't coupled right and it ran over him and crushed him.

I was stunned yet I somehow made it through my shift. It occurred to me that I didn't know his last name. Hell, I didn't even know his real first name. To me my pal was simply Red.

These shape-up jobs lead to feature writing for magazines. One afternoon after I'd finished work some where I was walking along Queen Street after being dropped off at the corner of Sherbourne. Coming toward me was the writer George Fetherling—or Doug as he was known then—with an older man he introduced as Robert Fulford. I kept up with Fulford's column and essays and admired him from a distance. The first thing he said to me after we were introduced was "Why are you dressed like that?"

I had on boots, jeans and a heavy shirt. I told him I'd been on a job. He asked questions and I explained about the shape-up. I'd been in the east end moving boxes and equipment around the floor of a machine ship. Fulford found this of interest and told me so. It was as if he'd never met anyone who had actually done anything like that.

He said, "Why don't you give me 2,500 words about it for the magazine?"

I thought this was great. I went back to my room and after dinner began writing the article. I brought it to the *Saturday Night* office on Monday morning and left it at the front desk. Fulford called me on Wednesday. "We're going to use it but, you know, you didn't have to do it so quickly. You could have taken a couple of months."

It was published a couple of months later and I had a big thrill one day in the basement of the old library when I saw a disheveled character reading my article and nodding his head appreciatively.

It wasn't so easy to get my next feature assignment. I queried all the magazines but it took a couple of years.

I got jobs banging nails and helping to put up fences, weeding flower beds and mowing lawns. The latter work gave me the idea to save for my own truck and start my own landscaping company. Although I never did go out on my own, I was reintroduced in landscaping and that lead to David Duplain and Geneva Gardens.

He was a good man and a good employer and I worked for him for parts of five years.

Being with a small landscaping outfit you get to do a wide variety of chores and your body goes through a wide range of motion every day. You pushed and lifted, bent and pulled. I worked in a lot of flower beds, getting to know flowers and ground covers, buses and shrubs. I had a mental block sometimes about names but I knew what to do with the plant. I got familiar with people's yards and flower beds, the impatiens were always where they were the last time. I knew exactly where I'd left off trimming the laurel hedge.

Then there were the home owners like the little bald man in North York who came out to tell you how a job should be done and the old woman in the big house on Oriole Parkway who watched you from behind the gauzy living room curtains.

In 1972 I made my first rip to the Yukon; my first day in Whitehorse I met a man who needed the insides of two houses painted. He hired me and I slept in the vacant houses every night for a week. Then I got another landscaping job. My first chore, and it would be one I'd do every week and a half, was to cut the weeds along the shoulders of the 12-mile paved section of the Alaska Highway within the Whitehorse boundaries. I did this, both sides of the road, on a tractor with harrow attachments.

I loved doing this but I had a hard time believing where I was and what I was doing. I was on the notorious road amidst that monumental scenery and I was just riding along, taking it all in and getting paid for it.

The next chore wasn't so much fun but the scenery was no less still breathtaking. This time the grass cutting attachment went on the tractor and I had to cut the grass at a power plant. Trouble was most of the property consisted of steep hills, and keeping the tractor, and me, from falling over was a nerve wracking chore.

Otherwise, most of the work was in a new suburban section of town called Riverside where it seemed everyone wanted a lawn just like people had down south, on the Outside. This entailed plenty of top soil spreading and sod laying. I didn't mind the shovel work, figuring it kept me in shape.

One of these jobs lead to me terminating my association with the Dutch guy. I was sent out to spread the top soil that he been delivered to the site. The next day I was to even out the soil and roll it prior to laying the sod.

I put in my eight hours and went home. The Dutch guy called me at night to complain that I hadn't even finished spreading the soil. "I worked all day with only time out for a sandwich and a coffee from my thermos."

"You only put down two and a half yards of topsoil. That shouldn't have taken you all day."

"There was a lot more than two and a half yards of topsoil waiting in that yard."

He denied this and hollered at me over the phone.

I told him to call the landscape supply place in the morning. When I got to the site in the next day he said he'd called the place and they had actually dropped off four yards of soil.

I waited for him to apologize for hollering at me but no apology was forthcoming.

"You really should apologize," I told him.

"I don't apologize to anyone."

"Well then I quit."

"You'll be sorry. Jobs are hard to find up here."

I walked away.

I hitch hiked to Dawson City where I met up with an old-Toronto friend, Erling Friis-Baastad. He'd had nearly as many dumb jobs as I'd had. Like me he needed the work but Erling was also a poet and he thought a nice list of jobs would look good on the back cover of a book. Of course, this was at a time when writers had jobs other than teaching creative writing.

Now he was working for Bob Cusick, a husky blond fellow who was connected to Yukon White Pass Route. His business was to load and unload planes at the Dawson City airport and deliver the goods to stores in town. Likewise, goods coming up from Whitehorse had to be loaded on the plane to Old Crow, the farthest north native Indian community in Canada.

There was box after box of plastic packages of Joe Louis (Joe Loueys) This was some marsh mellow-like sandwich of gooey white matter between slightly firmer brown matter. Joe Loueys were big in Old Crow.

Everything was shipped via the extensive YWPR system that included trains and boats and trucks and planes.

I kept working for Cusack until the end of August when an interesting assignment came to me from out of the blue. A German acquaintance in Toronto found out I was in the Yukon and could be reached via General Delivery, Dawson City.

Like many Germans, he was interested in Western history. He like so many others he had gotten hooked via the epic novels of Karl May. And if you're interested in the Yukon you have to pay attention to Gold. Bernard had begun to represent German investors with an even greater interest in Yukon gold. They had discovered information about an old Yukon town that used to exist out at the confluence of the original gold bearing creeks, Bonanza and Eldorado.

Bernard hired me to go and investigate the site and gather any information I could. The settlement which eventually had a population of ten thousand had begun because it was close to the source of the original discovery that started the Klondike Gold Rush. It was a boom town for a few years, an alternative to expensive, over crowded Dawson and the overworked local creeks.

Grand Forks flourished until 1904 when gold was discovered around Nome, Alaska and another rush began.

No one in Dawson seemed to know anything about Grand Forks. Even the people at the archives were unfamiliar with its history. I managed to find a few old newspaper articles and that was it.

So, I journeyed out to the old town site but all I found were warped boards scattered around, and two Germans. This couple, a man and a woman, were a fount of information about Grand forks. Everything they knew, they had learned back home in Dusseldorf. It was hard to imagine that where these warped grey boards lay on the ground where once electric lights and a population of ten thousand.

I took photographs and camped overnight among the old

boards and the remains of a stone wall. The night was as dark and the stars as bright as any young man camping out under them could wish. I headed back to Dawson in the morning and mailed my report to Toronto.

Bernard paid immediately and after I cashed the cheque I flew back to Toronto.

One afternoon I was walking around the Annex and there coming toward me was none other than my buddy Marcel Horne. After we made quick work of the preliminaries, he said, "I have a great gig. I'm Super at a Duplex on Howland Avenue."

"Don"t tell me," I answered. "Fifty-four or Fifty-six?"

"What! How do you know." I went back there with him. He was living in my old room. A couple of days later I was living on the other side of the wall from him and doing the Super chores at 56.

Marcel complained about the Greenbaum brothers and I took him down to Weiner's Hardware and soon we were both gathering inflated receipts and renting rooms to unusual characters. He had a Korean poet who hollered his poems in the middle of the night and a Japanese guy who had sex with his girl friend every night, their mattress being on the floor being next to the heating vent. Nothing so unusual about that except that the girlfriend was a screamer. And soon, the other roomers began to complain. At three in the morning, you were liable to be woken either by the Korean emoting or the Caucasian girl friend hollering in ecstasy, or sometimes both of them simultaneously.

But my favourite tenant was Jack Gummerson, a forty-year- old former tinsmith, now a full-time boozer.

Jack was a lanky six-foot tall fellow with lank straight brown hair. If he was having a happy day he'd begin to sing in the back yard; and was always the same song, and he sang it over and over, "Raindrops Keep Falling On My Head."

If it was a sunny day, Jack lay there on his back looking up at the blue sky and you could hear him singing and birds singing. Whether he inspired them or vice versa I never determined.

Jack had a unique way of supplementing his welfare cheques. In the late evenings, if he was only semi-drunk he would prowl the neighourhood looking for sagging rainspouts. If they didn't look about to collapse, he'd give them a little encouragement.

The next morning stone sober, and lank hair combed back in

his 1950s rockabilly style, he'd casually stroll by the houses whose rainspouts were lying in the yard, stop, rub his freshly shaven chin and 'tsskk, tsskk!" for the benefit of the home owner who had just discovered his misfortune. If no one was outside, Jack knocked on the front door and announced he had just been walking past the house when he noticed the rainspout had been torn from its anchors. Well, it just so happened he was a tinsmith and could make everything right.

To my surprise he would show up on time and do the work professionally. A couple of times he slipped me a few bucks to give him a hand lugging the spouts and drain pipes.

He usually didn't take a drink until the job was done. Usually. But he got a big job on the east side of Howland and a couple of blocks north of where we lived. He had to climb a ladder to the second-floor overhang and tend to the drain pipes on the third floor. He started up the ladder with an unopened bottle in his coat pocket.

One he was settled up there, he had his first drink and his second, Jack started singing "Raindrops" on a sunny day. Along about the fourth drink, he later told me, he got the idea to stay up there, maybe for good, so he kicked the ladder over fortunately killing no one and just missing a couple of cars at the curb. He gathered quite a crowd, men and women shouting at him and little kids laughing and cheering him. Eventually, the fire department appeared on the scene and Jack allowed himself to be carried down a ladder. He hit the ground smiling.

The shape ups at Queen and Sherbourne lead to me writing feature articles for magazines. I was coming home from moving equipment around a machine shop late one afternoon when I ran into the writer George Fetherling, or 'Doug' Fetherling as he was known then.

He was walking my way with an older balding man. We greeted each other and he introduced his partner as Robert Fulford. I knew Fulford's writing, I his columns and especially liked his 'Marshall Delaney' movie Pieces.

"Why are you dressed like that?" Fulford asked.

I had on jeans, a flannel shirt and lace up boots.

I told him and he asked questions about the work and the shape up. It was as if he had never actually met anyone who did that sort of thing.

"Why don't you give me 2,500 words on it for the magazine.?"

He was editor of *Saturday Night Magazine*.

Well, I was very pleased at his suggestion. I went home, had dinner and started writing the piece. I finished it late that night, typed up a clean copy the next morning and took it to the *Saturday Night* offices on Monday. A couple of days later Fulford telephoned to say they were going to use it.

"But you could have waited a couple of months to hand it in."

Soon I received a cheque in the mail. I thought his feature writing would open up an entirely new world for me. I queried other outlets for work but none was forthcoming. In fact, it was more than two years before I had another article published.

The *Saturday Night* piece did, however, lead to my first writing thrill. I was in the basement of the old library on College Street reading the *Los Angeles Times* when I heard a voice call out "Right on!"

I looked up and saw a street guy with *Saturday Night.* I casually drifted over and saw he was reading my article.

It was not long after this that I went to a Valentine's Day party and met an artist and photographer named Myfanwy Phillips. We began a romance that would last several years.

I was working for David Duplain in those days. Myf and I both liked country music and a big song of the day was Ronny Milsap's "I'm having Day Dreams About Night Things (in the middle of the afternoon)" with the line "While my hands make a living, my mind's home loving you."

I'd think of that while bent over in someone's yard with my hands in the dirt.

Myv was born in India and grew up in Malaysia and England. She was not pleased about living in Canada and wanted to go to the States about which she had romantic visions. We crossed the border into New York state and headed west. In Texas she expected the landscape would be filled with cowboys on horseback. We went into San Antonio and she was surprised there weren't hitching posts out of front of drinking establishments which were called 'bars' and not 'saloons.'
It was a long, leisurely trip and when we got to California headed directly to San Francisco.

We were near broke by the time we got there. We came to rest in Santa Barbara and began looking for work. She lucked into a job house and animal sitting for the woman who owned the Cougars used in the Mercury ads. The woman also had a piece of property where she kept a few more cougars, a camel and a couple of timber wolves. But Myv had nothing to do with these beasts, minding only the dogs at the woman's house.

I went to the California Employment agency and gave myself a Social Security number. I got a few days landscaping work with a crew, followed by a few days picking avocados; It was the hardest picking job I ever had or would ever have. The fruit had to be grabbed off the ground as soon as it fell from the tree or it would rot. The problem with this was that you put the avocados in a canvas sack, like an old mail bag, and as you worked the bag got heavier and heavier until you had fifty or sixty pounds hanging from your neck.

I got lucky with my next assignment. At the agency they told me an old movie star was looking for someone to pretty up his property in Montecito. But. They said, they don't want anyone who wants to go into the movies, no would be actors.

Well, that was me. I went out to the man's house and he turned out to be my childhood favourite western TV star, Duncan Reynaldo who played the Cisco Kid. He might have been a little wary at first but it didn't take long for him to accept me and soon we were friendly. He was a short husky man with deeply tanned or naturally dark skin and thick snow-white hair. I thought he'd look Mexican and he might have been but he had one of those faces, like Charles Bronson, that would have allowed him to play Hungarians or Portuguese or Indians as well as Mexicans and your generic pirate. He told me he didn't know his nationality, and had never known it. His first memory was being with some people he assumed were his parents but were not.

He had some palmettos in his front yard and a beautiful century tree. I cut the grass with an old-fashioned streamlined push mower.

After the first couple of days Reynaldo invited me to sit with him on the porch and have a cocktail. It became an after work ritual. I worked for him for two weeks, the last couple of days being sort of make work, doing chores that didn't really need doing. Finally he told me money was getting tight. He liked having me around but couldn't afford to pay me. If I hadn't been just scraping by I would have gone out there just to hang around with him.

Although I never asked him about the movies, I did tell him that as a kid, I watched 'the Cisco Kid' religiously.

As I was leaving the last day, he said, "Jimmy do you want to do that bit?"

I knew immediately what he meant, and exclaimed "Oh, Ceesco.!"

And Duncan Reynaldo replied, "Oh, Pancho!"

All this time, except when I could get out to the Cougar lady's house in the hills, I was staying in town, first at a mission on a cot on the in the midst of fifty other guys.

At night, in addition to the thunderous snoring, there would be screams as men relived Vietnam experiences in their dreams.

When I got a few bucks together from working, I took a room at a skid row hotel called the Neal. I put in a couple of days scraping and painting a boat down at the harbour, then got sent to my best gig of all.

"That old actor gave you a good report, said you never hassled him about getting into films so we want to send you out to the home of another old actor. He needs someone to Paint his house and clean up his yard. He's a well-known character around town."

The house of this man was on Torremolinos Drive, a one-story rancher with Spanish overtones. My first sighting of Jack Donovan, one-time silent screen star, he was stepping down from his front steps and onto a lawn of baked brown grass. In one arm he was cradling a plaster statue of the virgin Mary and holding a wooden pole with an American flag in the othert He looked in my direction and called, "Is that you, Roy?"

No," I called back. "I'm Jim from the employment agency." Just then a tall, bald, raw-boned man came striding from the side of the house. As he passed me he said, "Stay away from him if you've got any sense. He'll just get you in trouble."

Donovan regarded me for a moment and asked, "Do you know who that was?"

"No, but he looks like Erich von Stroheim's ugly twin brother." Donovan smiled and nodded his head, "Von Stroheim, knew him well. What a fake. He was no German count who deserved a 'von.' He was a Jewish man from _____."

I nodded as if I'd known it all along.

The man introduced himself and invited me into the house. He seemed mystified at the notion of me painting his house. He shook his head, "I have other more important work for you."

"Okay."

"First tell me how you know what Erich von Stroheim looked like."

"I keep my eyes open."

He laughed and nodded.

"Can you drive?"

"Yes."

"Good you're going to be my chauffer. We'll show them."

"Show who what?"

"Show the authorities, particularly the minions of the law that this is one guy they can't push around any longer. Are you in?"

"Is that your baby blue 1960 Cadillac in the driveway."

"Yes, it is."

He said it was and I said, "I'm in."

His 'study' looked like the site of a jumble sale. Three desks were stacked with papers. Lamps and antiques sat on shelves and a heavy mahogany table but it was the framed photographs that most attracted my attention.

"Hey, that's Jean Harlow," I said. "Who's that with her?"

"That's me. We were an item for awhile. Quite a dame, she was."

"You were in movies?"

"Yeah, I as mostly what they called a 'Juvenile Lead" which meant a young man not a silly kid like it does now.

I played gangsters and cowboys and was the lead in a movie about a young guy hopping freight trains. I hopped a freight train myself to come out here from St. Louis where I grew up. I'm a cousin of Wild Bill Donovan."

He pointed to a few more photographs

"That one's Lila Damita, girl friend of Errol Flynn. Whenever they had a fight, Lila would call me and I went over there to comfort her. Flynn would just take off.

"   Anyway, my mother married the owner of the St. Louis Post Dispatch but not too long after the ceremony he died and I invited her to come out. When she said she was coming I built her a house."

"You built her a house?"

"Yeah I was an architect, too. Introduced what they call French windows to America. I designed the Santa Monica yacht club. He pointed to a photo from the Twenties of a man standing by a roadster with a couple of big dogs on the running board. In the background was a fancy Spanish looking pile and a sign: "This is the house that Jack Built."

And you see this guy here?"

He pointed to another photograph of two men in white suits, their hair parted in the middle.

"That's me and old Burroughs."

He didn't mean William S. but Edgar Rice.

"He wanted to put together a big development and call it Tarzana. I designed it for him. Interesting fellow. But that house, a mansion really, that I built for my mother I eventually sold it to Mae Murray a silent screen star you probably never hear of. She wanted me with the deal but I was going with Clara Bow, the redhead. Mae Murray sued me or alienation of affection, and I counter sued. It was my first foray into the corrupt legal system.

"What you have to do before we start driving is get me on nation wide television. People have to know all about the corrupt judges out here. You better sit down and call Marv Griffin."

Jack told me that people were trying to take advantage of him because he was old. He said he was eighty but resembled one of those sixty-year old California heath nuts and gym rats.

"They took my daughter away from me. I got to get even."

"When did they take her away from you?"

"Last year."

This I didn't understand. A daughter of his had to be fifty or more. How could authorities take her away from him?

"How old is you daughter?"

"She's eight how."

"Eight?"

"Yes. And my son, they railroaded him into Chino."

Chino is a prison.

"I have to go down there. How about going with me tomorrow?"

"Sure thing, Jack."

"I like your attitude, kid."

We went to Chino with the top down. I waited in the Cadillac while Jack went in to visit his son. It was the first of our many trips together. We must have become a familiar sight on the Southern California freeways. While I drove, he'd sit in the backseat eating dried figs and apricots and sipping oat or goat's milk. His customary attire consisted of yachting shoes, loose white slacks, white shirt, blue blazer and a yachting cap. Tufts of white hair protruded from cap. He wanted me to wear a yachting cap "So we'll look like a team;"

"Sure, and how about we get matching short sleeve shirts with our first names embroidered over the breast pocket."

It didn't take long for me to realize that he was obsessed with the legal system. We'd be going along on a beautiful day under a smog-free blue sky and Jack would be talking about Rudolf Valentino or Rex Ingram, then suddenly interrupt himself to fulminate about some judge in Encino.

Under his direction I supplied myself with various fake letters of introduction and false identification documents.

I had a nice letter from an editor at Esquire magazine asking whomever it might concern to facilitate my research. We visited the Los Angeles Times and I even penetrated the inner sanctum of Standard Oil, allowing myself to feel just a little like Sir Richard Francis Burton getting into Meccah.

I remember driving around Los Angeles one afternoon listening to his story about his old friend, Charles Bickford, the actor. When Bickford was nine years old, a streetcar driver ran over and killed his dog. The kid went home, got his father's revolver, waited for streetcar and shot the driver.

Bickford was a romantic lead in his early acting days but then he got mauled by a lion and because of extensive scarring to his neck was relegated to character parts.

Back on Torremolinos Drive one afternoon, I was puttering around and house while Jack watched television. "Wow!" I heard him explain, "Look at that dame!"

There was a woman singing as she stood by a piano that was being played by a man in a Greek fisherman's cap.

"Look at her back! Who is she?"

"That's Toni Tenille and the guy is her husband, he's called the Captain."

"Well never mind him. I have to have that dame. You have to get in touch with her for me."

"Yeah, right. She'll be only too glad to talk to me on the phone and let me set up a rendezvous for the two of you."

"You better get to it."

Well, I had much better luck getting through to Toni Tenille than I did to Merv Griffin. It took me the rest of that Afternoon and most of the next day but then suddenly, there was her husky voice on the phone. I explained what I was about. Jack on the edge of his chair, had even taken off his yachting cap out of respect.

"He's over eighty years old now but he's still spry and he used to be a popular actor. He was in sixty movies. A very nice man. I wonder if you would do me the favour of just saying to word or two to him. His name's Jack Donovan."

"… No, he doesn't want to speak to the Captain."

Well, they had their brief conversation and he made it clear that he could come up to Studio City to visit and she was always welcome to fall by the place on Torremolinos.

Before that incident I got along fine with Jack; after it, I could do no wrong. In fact, Jack dug me enough that, he enlisted me to serve as his character witness in an upcoming trial at the Santa Barbara courthouse.

So, there I was a Canadian citizen pretending to be an America, a resident of Santa Barbara having moved here from the East Coast. I forget the reason for the court appearance. Someone, a guy a few years older than me, had some trouble with Jack and had him arrested.

I told the judge that I'd always known Jack as an upstanding member of the community and a paragon of honesty and integrity. I followed the script and told how we'd met when I was doing some repairs at the Casa del Mar, a house he had built in Beverley Hill

Jack showed me an article in an old movie magazine, *Photoplay*. I believe, raving that besides being an actor and architect he worked regular stints as a lifeguard at Santa Monica. "A dynamo of energy" the magazine called him.

Jack was worried about the outcome of the hearing. He was renowned as a rascal in a town that didn't take kindly to rascals. Also, he had been before the court the year before, charged with operating a stolen bicycle ring. He was supposed have had kids stealing bicycles for him to sell. He claimed to have had nothing to do with such nonsense. It was obvious that the judge and, indeed, everyone around the courthouse and most people in Santa Barbara looked at him as a nuisance and trouble maker but Jack emerged unscathed from this particular legal imbroglio less because he was innocent -what did that have to do, with it?—than because the guy laying the charges was an obnoxious punk.

I had been spending most nights in Jack's spare room but one evening I went back to the Neal in time to discover a guy in my room going through my cloth bag.

I knew the fellow. He didn't look like anyone's idea of a nut case but he was. I didn't hit him or rough him up in anyway, I just escorted him firmly from my room. I'd first run into him on the beach. He was going through the motions of a pitcher on the mound. His chubby white legs protruded from madras shorts. He toed an imaginary rubber, went into a windup and threw an imaginary baseball.

His name was Billy Ives; he was forty-two years old and had deserted his wife to get a head start on Spring training. When he got in shape and thought his fastball was hopping, Billy was going to head across country with Greyhound to join the Boston Red Sox camp at Fort Meyers, Florida.

Billy was flabby and forty-two and had never played organized ball but he was sure the Red Sox would sign him up once they saw his stuff.

He'd be a major leaguer then and have a lot of money to send home to his wife.

I wonder if he ever got there, and if he ever did, I hoped the Red Sox treated him civilly.

Myv's stint in the hills with the Cougar lady was coming to an end and she was restless to get back to work in Toronto. I was going to miss old Jack Donovan and I called him from a bar in town called the "Fred C. Dobbs"

That was the name of Humphrey Bogart's character in *Treasure of the Sierra Madre*. When I first saw Jack and learned he'd been in films, I pictured him playing Fred C. Dobbs. He also could have been the John Huston gringo who Dobbs was always hitting up at the beginning of the film.

I told him I was leaving

"No, kid," he said. "You can't leave. We have a lot to do."

We have to straighten out these judges down here and then we'll make a picture together. I still have plenty of contacts. Stick around, kid. There'll be money in it.

"Ah, Jack. You're conning me."

He didn't say speak for a long moment, the he said, "Well maybe a little bit."

I laughed.

"It's been fun though, hasn't it?"

"Sure has, Jack."

"*Vaya con Dios.*"

"*Hasta luego.*"

"So, we went to Toronto; Myv happy to be getting back to familiar territory, not that she liked the city but she had her friends there and her art table. I worked at a machine shop on Cherry Street and did some free lance writing.

We had to get some money together for future trips so I went looking. What ensued were a couple of the strangest jobs I've ever had, ones the I couldn't then nor can I now, get a handle on .I answered an ad in the star placed by a Jewish man who lived way up at the north end of Bathurst Street. He needed someone to clip stories from the newspapers, not all the stories just the ones who mentioned the names of his clients or their products or businesses.

His little apartment was stacked with papers; He took all the local dailies and weeklies as well as the Ottawa papers and whatever American ones he could get hold of.

The stacks of papers reminded me of skyscrapers and I was some giant striding down the streets. I liked the man; he reminded me of Monte Wooley speaking Yiddish.

He had hired me only because his back was giving him problems. "The back is why I don't believe in God," he told me.

"You'll have to explain that one."

"It's a design flaw. Everyone gets a sore back. We were made to walk bent over."

"We couldn't do that because our backs are too straight. And our arms too short."

"Precisely. And we'd look pretty funny going down Bathurst like that."

After four or five weeks he felt well enough to put in more time, and needed to save the money he was paying me so that was that.

By the time winter rolled around Myv and I had scraped enough money together to escape to warmer climes. For us that meant Florida.

With my fake Social Security number and a fake name, I got a part time job at the Ripley's Believe It Or Not Museum in St. Augustine. But Myv and I had been growing apart. Neither of us was to blame, we just had different interests. She moved to Ormond Beach, a little north of Daytona. And I rented a trailer on the Boulevard, across from The Spanish Armada, my favourite watering hole. And the Armada was next door to the Spanish restaurant where I'd washed dishes.

Myv was sewing some wild oats in Ormond Beach and I eventually took up with a dark complexioned, black-haired, part Mexican woman, Mary Anne Silva.

I rented an office in the Atlantic Bank Building on the town square that used to be the slave market and there I wrote my book about the Alaska Highway and the territory it passes through.

Saint Augustine didn't look like other towns in Florida. It had been founded by Minorcans from Spain in the early Sixteen hundreds, and the Spanish influence was everywhere and natural, not laid on like in other

Florida towns like Boca Raton. There were still houses standing from the earliest times, in fact, St Augustine is the oldest continually inhabited town in North America.

It had an aura of sophistication lacking in most of the rest of the state and it was beautiful but it was still a southern town with all the prejudice that implies.

There was a short, stocky and very black man of indeterminate age who used to dance jigs and bum quarters in the Square. I can still hear him plead, "Godda qwahdah, Mister?"

College boys, especially from up north got a charge out of him, clapped and threw change which he scuttled about plucking from the ground while the white folks laughed. Every day could have been a hundred years before.

The old Fort dominated the waterfront; it had once held Geronimo, a man of the desert trapped in a tiny cell in the Florida humidity.

When Spring rolled around, I was ready to head north and get on with David Duplain's outfit..

When I first got with David, he and Ria lived on Lonsdale Avenue north of downtown. After a year or so they bought a house in West Hill east of Scarborough. West Hill was to be the site of the new zoo and I spent days driving loads of fill to the side in a rented dump truck. The procession of similar vehicles seemed to go on all day long, and probably did.

Although I still liked the work, getting to David's new location took nearly two hours. I'd catch the subway on Bloor Street at the St. George stop and ride it east to the end of the line. From there I transferred to a bus for the last half hour of the commute.

He hired another employee, a blond-haired guy who was studying to be a lawyer. I forget his name but he is the only fellow worker I didn't like. He was prissy and forever reporting back to the boss about things that might have been done better. He specialized in what he considered to be faults in my driving technique, although he didn't drive himself.

One man David hired was an interesting fellow named Terry Kline who had studied herbal medicine in China and was a devotee of big band music. I liked working with him and several years later we'd meet up in Vancouver and did landscaping there.

I occasionally got work for my friends. Marcel put in a few days but didn't care to do anything but drive and fix equipment, consequently there was always some equipment that needed to be fixed.

Another fellow I arranged to work for David was Barry Dickie. I'd met Barry at 56 Howland Avenue. He was a tall and lanky raw-boned guy who answered the ad Marcel put in the paper advertising a room for rent. Marcel had inserted a line about 'creative type' preferred.

When Barry showed up he admitted he wanted to write but hadn't done much of it. Marcel then asked if he smoked dope. When Barry answered in the affirmative Marcel told him, "Well, that's creative enough."

Barry was a likeable stand-up guy who at the time described himself a "a cab driver of no particular distinction, no girl friend and limited social skills.".

He was a good, dependable worker and David appreciated his help. Barry worked on and off for Geneva Gardens until he hired on as a gardener with the city, a trade he pursued until he retired in 2016.

During these years whenever I got enough money together, I'd go off on a trip. I went to Europe several times in the Seventies and to the Amazon four times.

One year. Hitchhiking in Switzerland, I got a ride from a fellow my age in a sleek sportscar. When Franz discovered I was as interested in cars and anarchism as he was, he invited me to come with him to the family home in the Jura Mountains. When I commented on the anarchist watchmakers of the Juras, he smiled. "You'll meet an old one."

He lived in a blood red wooden chalet with a sharp pointed roof in a narrow valley, called a Cluse, between two mountain peaks. Also living in the big house was his grandfather, his mother, a girl I took to be his girlfriend and a young statuesque Nubian woman. There were goats and chickens, an old cow and an older Audi in the barn.

When Franz told him I knew something about anarchism the old fellow perked up, firing names as me, such as Hippolyte Havel; he was surprised not only that I knew of him but had read a book of essays by the old-time anarchist.

"And what have you read of Kropotkin, young man?"

"I've read *Mutual Aid* and *the Conquest of Bread*."

"Ah, we were friends he and I and my wife. We'd have him over to the house and he'd sit in that very chair where you're sitting.

I can't explain the feeling I got learning that the great man had put his arms on these same arm rests. I couldn't have cared less where George Washington or Napoleon sat or slept but to me but was an honour to be sitting where a truly great man had sat.

Well I was then invited to stay as long as I wanted.

"And you can have that old Audi."

Soon I was driving around with Franz, delivering milk and a watch or two. The grandfather had spent his working life as a watchmaker but he didn't do much of that nowadays because his eyesight was failing.

One night the old man looked from me to Franz and shook his head. "You two could be milk brothers."

When we weren't out driving around, I cleaned up the barn, fed the animals, tinkered with the Audi and talked to the Nubian girl.

The situation was almost idyllic. 'Almost' only because I was restless. It seemed too easy somehow and I had to be going.

Finally, Franz drove me out of the mountains and left me off on a main road. I was downhearted but I waved goodbye and hitchhiked to Paris.

Later, in Vancouver, I heard the Green peace was looking for fund raisers. And they hired me as a door to door solicitor. I went around selling memberships and magazines on a commission basis. This turned out to be quite profitable. The company realized I was signing up quite a lot of new members so they sent me into areas thought to be resistant to Greenpeace and its ideas, certain Vancouver suburbs, such as Coquitlam and Port Moody.

I'm not boasting when I state that I brought in nearly twice as much money as the next canvasser. There was no secret to it as my supervisor found out when he went with me one evening. The bosses had begun to believe I must be doing something unethical or making outrageous promises.

The man followed me on my rounds and was surprised to see everything was above board. "I don't get it," he said. "How come they give you money don't give to anyone else?"

"It's simple," I explained. "I look more like them. In other words I don't show up knocking on their doors with dirty clothes and matted hair. My expression doesn't give them the idea I resent them for living in the suburbs and having regular jobs."

The powers that be wanted to recruit me to participate in various demonstrations and confrontations. I went to a couple of planning sessions but they were too much like military briefings.

One plan was to disrupt the Japanese consulate because of whaling activities. Their intention was to 'fight' their way on to the roof and drape fishing nets over the sides. They also talked of throwing red paint around but I didn't know this at the beginning. I told the bosses that we could just walk in there, I'd hand them my business card from *Vancouver Magazine* they'd let us go up on to the roof. There were three of us. In the lobby I announced myself and showed my card. I said I was doing an article and we rode the elevator to check out the view from the roof for photo possibilities.

They let us go up and we looked around and I handed around my card. I did actually have an idea in mind: a Greenpeace operation from the inside.

The event was to take place in six weeks. In the meantime I took a trip to Fiji. Upon my return I learned that I was in trouble. The provacateurs had gone in, created a disturbance, thrown the paint around and scattered my cards all over.

The Japanese were angry at me and so was *Vancouver Magazine*. The latter never gave me another assignment.

The Greenpeace Higher-ups explained that had they not made such a fuss, the 'Cause' wouldn't have gotten publicity.

It seemed self-righteous and childish. I resigned.

I started getting more interesting and better paid magazine assignments. The first job that I received expenses for was a piece on mercenary soldiers. There were more than a few Canadians involved in this trade. I went to Sandhurst in London and the arms factories of Ostend, Belgium.

After that one, I seemed to be able to go wherever I wanted. I covered the fighting in Rhodesia and South Africa; Nicaragua and El Salvador. With my expenses paid I was able to get to other places on side trips, too, for instance, Namibia and Swaziland.

There were grandiose plans afoot for a Trans-Amazonian Highway and I wanted to explore what was going on. I had been to the Amazon once before and that was a good trip to have on my resume when I asked the mag azine to send me to Brazil. When they gave their assent, I remember distinctly going to the travel agent in St. Augustine to get my ticket. She was a large middle-aged woman with frosted hair, cats-eye sunglasses and white fingernails.

"Is this your first trip to the Amazon?"

"No; my second."

"I've been there twice," she said.

It was a sort of golden age for freelance journalism in Canada. You could receive expenses and get paid decently for the stories you handed in. Years later when I would talk about this to younger journalists they found it hard to believe. When the purse strings began to tighten, I was frequently able to arrange a complimentary ticket with an airline or tourist board, this with the promise of a relevant article. In this way I got to Australia, Fiji, New Zealand and Greenland. The only travelers to Greenland had been fishermen but for a few months you could catch a flight from the Canadian military base called CARP which was near Ottawa. The plane took you to Nuuk or Gothab, the capitol. While there I earned a few bucks or, rather, a few beers, appearing in a rock video. I had never even seen a music video. I met some Inuit musicians in a bar and we got along. Then they invited me to play the typical uptight Danish business man in the film We went out on to an iceberg in the harbour. I sat at a card table before an old typewriter, pretended to type and then yanked the paper from the roller, balled it up and tossed it away in frustration. I did this several times while in guys in the band jumped around and made like they were playing their guitars. The cords of their amplifiers were stuck into snow drifts.

The fruitful freelancing life continued steadily for five or six years when most outlets went out of business or decided to be entirely 'Canadian' which meant not acknowledging the outside world. They called this Nationalism.

About this time, Myv and I finally parted company. She stayed in the U.S. and I went back to Canada, only this time to the West Coast.

I hit Vancouver in the midst of housing crisis. Unable to find a place to live, I went to Salt Spring Island. Mary Anne joined me and we rented a house at Fulford Harbour. My plan was to hole up and write my biography of Charles Bedaux, the rags to riches millionaire business man, inventor and adventurer who hosted the wedding of the Duke of Windsor and Wallis Simpson and was unjustly accused of treason to the U.S. Bedaux also devised a system of work management that was erroneously called a speed-up plan. Bedaux would go into a business and advise owners how it could operate more efficiently. He was never one of those cartoon characters hiding behind a post in the factory timing workers with a stopwatch.

For instance, at the beginning of talking pictures in Hollywood, much time was lost by actors and technicians tripping over electric cords sprawled across the floors of sound stages. Bedaux spent one morning looking around and came up with the boom mike. He'd go into a factory and tell management to move the loading ramps.

I worked on my book but I was soon bored on Saltspring. One evening I took an orange sheet of poster paper and divided it into three by five pieces on which I stated that I would do lawn work and odd jobs. I left the house at nine the next morning to put them in mail boxes. I had bought a twelve year-old Chrysler for thirty five dollars. It had been standing in a field, the trunk occupied by chickens. I replaced the chickens with rakes and shovels and a lawn mower and was ready to deal with the deluge of phone calls that had come in while I was driving around. Mary Anne was angry, "I don't know what you promised them but the phone hasn't stopped ringing."

And there I was less than a week after leaving Toronto, hacking weeds at an ocean front property while seals watched me from the rocks.

It had been my idea to hopefully get ten hours work a week but I could have worked ten hours a day seven days a week. Besides cutting down weeds and mowing lawns, trimming bushes and pruning flowers, I was cutting and stacking firewood. As well I was contacted by absentee landlords who wanted someone to check on their rental properties.

There was no way I could begin to do all the work so I amazed myself by hiring someone. There were a lot of jobs to be filled on Salt Spring but few people wanted to fill them. The guy I hired had long hair and I took him to be a hippy, but most young guys on Salt Spring were hippies.

We went out to the first property which needed mowing. After showing him around, I asked him to cut the lawn while I'd go down the road to take care of another place.

When I got back a couple of hours later, he was lying on his back on the lawn smoking a joint. No work had been done. When I asked him why he hadn't done anything, he said, "Don't be uptight man. Be cool."

"Okay, I'll be cool. You just lie there and when your done the joint get yourself to Ganges."

"You owe me money, man."

"What for you? You didn't do anything."

"You owe me for my time."

I shook my head, walked to the Chrysler and drove off, leaving him to figure out his own way home.

I was so desperate for help that I telephoned my brother who had gotten married and was living in Montreal. He agreed right away to come out and help me, and arrived within a few days which should have made me suspicious.

Unlike the hippy he at least went through the motions of working. After a couple of weeks of his desultory 'help,' I asked him what was going on, why had he come out west.

"I'm sorry. I just had to get away."

He flew back to Quebec, and Mary Anne and I found a place to live in Vancouver. I needed access to libraries to finish my Bedaux book. It seems that nearly everyone in Vancouver in the Eighties was working in the movies. American film and tv companies were always shooting, and consequently there was always work. I got involved by chance when I accompanied James Iwasuk to an audition. He didn't get the part but he was given an extra role. The assistant director said he could use me, too. The film was *The Adventures of Natty Gann*. My bit was to sell doughnuts from a cart on the street. Vancouver's Mainland Avenue was standing in for a street in Chicago in the Depression.

At one point, Scatman Carothers is walking down the street, looks over at my cart and shouts, "Are your doughnuts any good, man?" I reply, "My doughnuts are out of sight."

I tossed him one which he caught deftly.

None of this was in the script. Whether it stayed in the movie, I don't know because I've never seen it but my cheque was for a lot more than the extra rate.

I sought out other movie work. I was in a couple of *22 Jump Streets* that starred Johnnie Depp. He was a snotty little guy who didn't even show up half the time.

After that I got extra bits in several episodes of *Wise Guys* and *McGyver*. Somewhere in in the midst of all this I got a magazine assignment in New Zealand. I explored some caves with a guide and one night went to dinner at his place. He had a twelve year old son who was awed when it came out that I actually been on a *McGyver* set and in close proximity to Anderson _____, the star. I promised the boy that I'd send him an autographed picture of the star if I ever got the chance.

Back in Vancouver I did get the chance but the star was reluctant to sign the 8 by 10 glossy, one of the publicity people gave me. He pretended to be too busy to take two seconds to sign his name.

I tried another time that day but got the brush off. Same thing next day. Finally I said, "Sign the Godamned thing. He's a kid and he looks up to you. Think of how he'll feel when I tell him you think you're too important to sign a photo". He gave me what he must have thought was a bad look but wouldn't sign. The publicity woman saved he day, "For chrissakes, _____; sign it."

I was a gunman on a movie shot in Ioco, on the edge of Vancouver. I let off several rounds on a submachine. The thing was filled with blanks and they'd pepper my face when ejected. One day in Ioco there must have been fifty people killed. I remember a stunt man being shot, toppling from a fire escape and and landing on the cardboard boxes set up below.

The next day at lunch I read the *Vancouver Sun,* which carried an interview with the movie's star, Dale Robertson. The old cowboy told the writer that the movie was good family entertainment, and that he would not hesitate to let his grand daughter watch it.

I began to be chosen for SOC—silent on Camera—work. This is sort of a glorified extra gig. You'll do a scene that requires direction but you don't have lines. On one show I had to assassinate a doctor. Previous attempts to eliminate him had failed. I got myself wheeled into the Intensive Care Unit on a gurney, feigning some accident or illness. The doctor came in and when his back was turned, I pulled out my IV tube and strangled him from behind.

Once I was a submachine gun terrorist on an airplane walking toward the camera with my weapon scanning the hostages.

A couple times I was a Russian. Most often, though, I was a Mob bodyguard. The main bad guy would stand talking to someone and I'd be beside him. my eyes arcing to look for danger. I did plenty of these. The pay was good.

I got with an agency but that didn't amount to much. I did go to an interesting audition for a role in a tv show. Every episode a couple of people appeared before a psychologist who listened to their problem. I did the audition with an older black man. The premise was that I was his rebellious son and he was my strict no-nonsense father. There was no script, we had to improvise.

The unlikely pairing was to test our ability to think on our feet. I got the part and appeared with an attractive woman who was supposed to be my wife. We were having marital difficulties which we made up on the spot. There were a couple of crew holding up signs off camera advising us what to talk about. One guy held up a sign that read SEX. My 'wife' picked up on it immediately and began complaining that I no longer showed any interest in her. She was all dolled up and taking advantage of her big opportunity on camera. "He never Wants to do it."

The fake audience, shook their heads at my failure. The woman shot me a look that meant, 'Try to get out of that one.'

I was intimidated for a moment. She wanted to be an actor but I didn't.

But I said to the doctor,, You look at her in that short skirt and stockings. Her high heel shoes. You notice the way she has crossed and uncrossed her legs, maybe five times in the last two minutes, and you're probably thinking, "She looks good. What's the matter with him?"

But this isn't what I see when I get home from putting in a full day at my construction job. Then she's wearing a baggy t-shirt with jam stains on it and a pair of sweat pants that've been through the washer and dryer a hundred times and have lint balls all over them. No high heels that's for sure but dirty old running shoes or those horrible crocs. Yeah, very sexy."

After we were done and had walked off the set. I said something about what we'd just done but she snubbed me and stalked off.

The show as broadcast live, and the next day as I walked along Robson Street I discovered the show was popular. People called to me about what they'd seen, assuming it was legitimate. One black guy yelled from the other side of the street, "Man, you got to ditch that bitch!"

It wasn't but a couple of minutes later that an elderly lady stopped me to offer some sincere advice, "Son, that woman just isn't not right for you. As difficult as it might be, you need to separate for your own good."

After that I did a commercial for an optometrist's shop. I was a guy in a white lab coat who showed different pairs of glasses to a patient/customer and made sure they fitted properly.

I had an acquaintance who was a plastic surgeon with a practice on Broadway in Vancouver. We'd met in a coffee shop, when he heard me telling someone about Guatemala. He revealed that he made so much money at his practice that he felt guilty and, therefore, every year he went down to Guatemala and operated on people with hare lips. He received no money for this.

"In Vancouver I make my living from people's vanity. I tend to a lot of actors and would be actors. There are young men who want the corners of their eyes lifted; women who want cat's eyes. The saddest of all are young guys who get their nostrils reshaped and made smaller. Of course, there are the usual lip enlargements, face lifts and tummy tucks. It's one thing when a sixty-year woman comes in for that sort of thing, but a twenty-five year old?"

I met a lot of these young guys at auditions; they almost reeked of vanity and ambition.

I got sent out on an audition for a western. My character was a 'trail bum' in his early or mid-forties. He's talking in a jail cell, hassling the sheriff.

There were four other guys at the audition. Only two of us were in our forties. The others were plastic surgery recipients who looked to be in their mid-twenties. The other fellow was over weight and had trouble saying his lines. When the audition was over, the casting director took me aside, "I'm sure you got it," she said. "The big guy is just too gross and the other ones are too young and pretty. I'll call you in the morning."

As I was leaving, the director nodded to me and smiled.
The casting director did call in the morning, only it was to tell me I didn't get the part.

"So, I guess the big guy got it."

"No, it was one of the blond guys."

"But they don't look like forty-year-old trail bums. They look like young golf pros."

"You're right but the Producer said, audiences don't want to see guys your age."

Well that just about did it for me. I had no acting ambitions to begin with. I figured there was no point to any of it. I did some work later but I hadn't gone looking for it.

I spent most of 2001 in Vietnam. I was living in Saigon and a local moto driver I knew stopped me on the street to say that a film company was looking for a westerner of a certain type and they were paying Thieu to bring them the right guy. I hopped on the back of his bike and we went out to the studio on the outskirts of the city.

They hired me immediately. It was a commercial for an electric foot massage device. I had to sit in a chair with my shoes and socks off and my feet on top of the flat machine. It was like a shallow box with metal wire-like cross pieces the thickness of a coat hanger. Small plastic disks were strung along the wires. When a switch was turned on the discs spun around.

So, I sat there being tickled by the little spinning disks. I had to talk while being filmed but I could say anything I wished. I went on about the two roads the blues followed when it came north from New Orleans, one road lead to Chicago, the other Kansas City, and how I preferred the more R and B and jazzy Kansas City style.

When they broadcast the spot, it carried an advertisement in Vietnamese characters across the bottom of the television screen. I wondered about the reaction of any English speakers viewing it and hearing me.

I did an audition in Saigon for an American soldier in what the

Vietnamese call The American War. The scene was set in a bar. I had to go up on stage and sing "Light My Fire."

I can't sing a little bit so I was surprised when I was offered the part. That's probably what they wanted: a guy who couldn't sing even a little bit Filming wouldn't start for two months, however, and I needed to get back to Canada.

I was led to believe I could get a lot of film work in Vietnam. They turned out a steady stream of movies and always needed Caucasians to play soldiers and diplomats.

I was only slightly tempted.

Back in Vancouver, I found another outside job, this with Willow Landscaping owed by another a husband and wife team, Ellen and Rob Macdonald. Rob had completed the well-respected gardening program at BCIT, the trade college in Vancouver.

Ellen was an experienced landscaper and gardener but she was also a new mother and I relieved her of the work.

I wasn't their first choice. They man they'd hired lasted three days before they fired him.

"We would have hired you first but we thought you knew too much and there'd be conflict?.

The only conflict we ever had was in the first hour of my first day at work. Rob snapped at me because he thought I closed the door of his van too hard. But apart from that there was never any problem.

There was new foliage to deal with on the Coast like banana plants, bamboo and palm trees. All of these presented their own problems.

People bought palm trees from a gardening centre, planted them and when they didn't grow for four years the home owner became annoyed. But these palm trees were in shock. They'd been dug out of the ground in California and shipped up to Canada where they sat in a gardening centre for who knows how long. The trees weren't going to grow at all for a few years. Often the home owner would get angry with Rob and I even though we hadn't planted the trees. We must have done something that prohibited their growth. The owner would claim we cut the grass too close to the trunk or planted the hydrangeas too close to the tree.

I worked for Rob and Ellen for three years and after that I moved to the Sunshine Coast and took care of my own customers. I

Made contact with a couple of tropical plant devotees who grew palms and nanas from seed, and I started planting these. As I sit here typing I can look out the window and across the road at a property that features a 25-foot-high palm tree and a New Zealand fern the same height. eighteen years ago I planted those at another place in town and when that house was sold the man across the street had them transplanted to his yard. They were grown from seed and the fern is the only one of its kind I've ever seen or heard of in Canada.

Bamboo is great to look at but it can cause endless problems. People plant it with no forethought. It proliferates incredibly and takes over gardens and lawns and after it has done so, people call the landscaper to get rid of it then can't understand why it takes so long to do so. The roots run deep and wide and to get rid of them you need all manner of cutting and chopping tools.

The only way to keep bamboo from running riot is to take precautions when it's planted. You need to dig a trench and set a sheet of metal into the ground to surround the new plants.

Some folks even put rugs down where they want to create a weed-free flower bed. They have top soil shovelled over the rug and put in their plants. This may keep weeds from sprouting but not being able to emerge into the light their tentacles spread laterally under the surface of the garden bed creating a tough fibrous mesh which is a nightmare to destroy. You can't chop it with an axe because the thin roots don't offer any resistance to the axe or whatever blade you try to use. Cedar chips are almost ubiquitous in B.C. flower beds. They may kill weeds but they are harmful to everything else because their high acid content deprives the soil of oxygen.

In two places were Willow called, the home owner distributed bones in the flower beds, the idea being that bone meal is good for growth. And the bones might indeed help but only when they break down which would take about seven hundred years. As well, the bones are packed with bacteria and parasites. It would help to bake them in the oven and crush them after a long period of boiling, but who wants to go through all that trouble.

Another thing people are fond of doing, is putting coffee grounds in the soil. There is absolutely no logic to this but the coffee grounds look like topsoil. Cotoneaster, a woody ground cover that sprouts pink flowers but also repels weeds, still the best way to get rid of weeds is to get down and pull them out by the roots.

I worked for Willow for three years until Rob and Ellen moved away.

Upon settling in British Columbia, I was struck by the different kinds of jobs my new friends had on their resumes as compared with those I knew back in southern, Ontario.

Back there you rarely meet a man who has been a logger or a lumberjack as they are called. Here ex-loggers are everywhere. The man in the next apartment was a logger as was the building's handyman.

Me, I never worked in the woods. By the time I settled out here logging was a dying industry and machines had taken over most of the jobs.

The closest I've gotten was at various times setting chokers to drag trees out of the bush.

Neither did I encounter commercial fishermen in Ontario unless they had migrated from the Atlantic provinces.

As for the writers I knew very few had ever done manual labour jobs of any kind. One exception was my pal Len Gasparini a one-time truck driver and warehouse worker who had done brief stint at the Dixie Brewing Company in New Orleans.

I gave up mentioning jobs to fellow writers because too often they figured I was playing the role of 'working class writer' or else researching an article.

Most had been office workers or taught in universities.

By contrast it seems that nearly every guy I meet on the Coast and many of the women have worked on fishing boats. My friend Gary Kent who I go hiking with, quit his good job as a Museum director, bought a boat and spent the rest of his career fishing for salmon.

He told me about work he had done prior to either of those occupations. As a young man in Vermillion, Alberta he delivered Coca Cola to small towns throughout the Province. "I stayed in cheap hotels and wandered around and met some interesting people. I went to rodeos and fell in with some ear biters. It's horse's ears they bite."

It seems that many rodeos feature Wild Horse Racing for which you need one horse and three men. The horse bursts from the chute and the shank man grips the halter; meanwhile another man grabs the horse's head, twists it and bite its ears; then, the third man, the rider throws on a saddle and races the horse to the finish line.

Ear Biter is not an occupation I would have wanted to pursue. It is more the kind of thing that would fit the resume of my unfortunately departed friend, the travel writer Garry Marchand who really had been everywhere. Garry once put in a few months as a mosquito counter in the highlands of New Guinea.

Steve Schwabel, is an actor and musician but he grew up learning the building trade from his father, and later worked on fishing boats all along the Inside Passage.

Jon van Arsdell, a tough little guy with a degree in ichthyology, was a fisherman and biologist on fishing boats. Philip Gaulin was a truck driver and mill worker.

Stu Young whom I mentioned as working in the Calgary warehouse with the fellow who slept through his shifts has had an interesting career. He was an all-around handy man, who did numerous jobs as a young man but suddenly quit that sort of life to become a librarian. Stu put in his years and retired at a relatively young age after which he went back to being a handyman.

My late buddy Peter Trower, known as 'the logger poet' spent twenty years in the woods and on the slopes doing every kind of job around trees except topping them. Pete produced dozens of poems about logging and mill work and about the dives and cheap hotels in Vancouver where loggers repaired between stints in the bush.

There have been several other poets who over the years who have produced logging poems and songs. A genre unknown in Ontario. Robert Swanson of Vancouver Island was a mechanic on donkey engines who wrote Robert Service influenced poetry. He also fabricated steam whistles. When diesel engines took over from steam locomotives in the late Fifties and early Sixties, it was discovered that people missed the haunting and romantic sounds of the old steam whistles. Swanson was given the task of replicating those sounds with diesel engines. In certain areas of Canada, the diesel whistles lead to collisions with wildlife which lead to train accidents and derailments. Moose, particularly, in Northern Ontario would charge the diesel locomotives with the new whistle which they thought were other moose challenging them.

Swanson's invention was so successful that soon every diesel had the new whistle. The moose were able to relax, too.

I have a friend named Karl O'Day. When I met him thirty years ago he was working in a wrecking yard in Vancouver and sleeping in a different vehicle every night. When I moved to the Sunshine Coast Karl was there and we did some jobs together. The worst, I recall, was moving rocks and boulders across a field to line a long driveway. Karl is seventy-nine years old now and until this year was still working four days a week in construction. I came across him one day climbing a ladder with shingles draped over his shoulders.

Karl has a deep, strong singing voice and now makes a living busking out of front of Liquor stores.

Office workers don't have stories to match those of working guys. My friend Jon van Arsdell tells of being a prison guard at an island detention centre. There was an inmate who was there for cattle rustling. Not only that but he'd had his drawn and quartered cow delivered to him by mistake. The thing is, it was the Mounties who delivered it.

Mountie stories abound on the West Coast, a famous one being about the time a store worker came home early from his shift and saw an RCMP cruiser in his driveway. Opening his front door, he saw a Mountie's uniform spread across his living room, including the Constable's boots and gun.

He heard noises coming from upstairs and there in the bedroom, in his marriage bed was his wife having sex with the Mountie. So intent were they on what they were doing, they didn't hear the husband who went back down the stairs as quietly as possible.

The man gathered up the Mounties uniform, his boots and his gun, and took them to RCMP headquarters where he deposited them on the counter.

It's rumoured that the Mountie was transferred to Northern Manitoba. Philip Gaulin laments days gone by when people had monikers. I recall old friends of mine called One Ball Freddy, Golf ball, Frisco Jack, Steam Shovel Scotty, and Big Girl Shorty not to be confused with Maggie Shorty of Britt, Iowa.

Anyway, there was a tall lanky guy who hung around Lower Gibsons who had an aversion to washing but always wore a stylish Frank Sinatra hat. In wintertime Lanky Pete would go from one business to the next lurking in heated vestibules for a little warmth. One afternoon, huddled in the vestibule of the Bank of Montreal, he got the bright idea to rob the place. He needed help so he rounded up a couple of other local layabouts and hatched his idea. Before the night of the robbery, Lanky Pete called an eleventh-hour meeting to go over the plan. But, alas, one of the conspirators had squealed to the Mounties who wired the guy for the meeting. One of the men expressed worry about fleeing the head Mountie, whose name was Sergeant Ruggles. Lanky Pete was caught on tape, stating: "Don't worry about Ruggles he couldn't track on elephant on the rag across the snow."

Lanky Pere got two years in Okalla. I'd like to think he had to spend that whole time listening to his cellmate Eddy Haymour going on and on about the injustices done to him.

Not long after I settled on the Sunshine Coast, I was too old to work in the woods or start at the Port Mellon pulp mill. I got a job at as janitor at a YMCA camp named for an incompetent British general. I had to clean the numerous washrooms twice a day, sweep and wash the dining room floor as well as the hallways.

There girls' and boys' dormitories, and outbuildings with toilets throughout the forty acre property. Let no one tell you that girls are cleaner than boys.

The kids ranged from twelve to eighteen and were from different countries: Canada, the U. S., Japan and Mexico. There were vast differences between them in terms of maturity.

A twelve year of Japanese kid was the equal of an eighteen-year-old American. I had my own standings for the kids. Canadians were saved from the bottom due to the presence of the Americans. The Mexicans were the most mature—but then they came from upper class families who could afford to provide them good educations and send them to camp in Canada. Next came the Japanese.

There was lots of hostility between the American and the Mexican campers, and the counselors were concerned that this state of affairs might lead to violence. But they but they had no idea bout why it existed. Since I could speak some Spanish I listened to conversations between the Mexicans and was able to discern that that the Americans looked down on the Mexicans, and trotted out all the old cliches about lazy peasants and dirty banditos. This naturally didn't still well with Mexicans. I think it is safe to say the Mexicans were twice as smart as the Americans. (Canadians were caught in a bind; they seemed to have an idea what was going on but most felt they had to align themselves with the American kids).

The counsellors resented me for trying to indicate what was going on. Afterall I was just the old janitor of all things trying to tell them what was going on.

The season at the camp ended in the middle of September but I was told I could stay on for another six weeks if I wished. I was kept busy giving everything a thorough last clean, maintaining the equipment that I had used.

I had a work mate. Bradley was a good worker and good companion. He had a speech impediment, however, and management ignored him. I was asked if I thought they should decline to rehire him for the next season because he didn't present a good image of the operation. I replied that they were lucky to have him.

Despite it being the latter part of November, I went out on my own when I was done at the camp, The coldest time of the year on the Coast is usually the middle of December, and that's the only time landscapers cease working outdoors.

But when January came around, I headed down to Mexico. Mary Anne and I spent our Luna de Miel in a town on the Pacific Coast and went back there, me driving us in an old Chevy I bought in Vancouver. It was a good trip down through Baja California and across the water by ferry to Mazatlan. When we got to our town, we rented a house on the slope looking out over the ocean. It was an ideal spot, the lighting was great and I was soon spending my time walking, swimming and doing art work. I had been going on and on about how I was going to paint. Finally, Mary Anne got tired of hearing me and gave me a package of beginners acrylics for Christmas.

From the beginning I spent more time at the art work than I did the writing.

I realized that I wanted another dimension and went from paintings to collage then on to assemblages. I also made figures out of driftwood with pebbles or seeds for eyes. Some of these sculptures had religious references.

The landlord who lived up the hill from us, sent his cleaning lady down to work at our place. She was a middle-aged Mexican woman. I noticed her looking carefully at my figures on the wall. Wen I saw her cross herself in front of certain of the pieces and I figured I might be on to something.

One afternoon, a couple of wealthy looking gringas came by the place thinking it was where an acquaintance of theirs lived. We invited them in anyway and they were drawn to the sculptures.

"They're great," one of them said. "Where did you get them?"

"I made them."

"Really?"

"Really."

It turned out they out a gallery in a government resort town not to far away.

"I think we could sell these in our shop."

The result of this visit to the wrong house was that they went away with three driftwood sculpture. A few days later, I ran into one of the gringas walking on the beach.

"Glad to see you," she said. "I have a cheque for you."

"You mean you sold one?" This was great news. I had never sold a piece of art before

"No," she said. "I sold all three."

Unfortunately, they didn't sell any more of them but the gallery display lead to an interesting job. I got a visit from a woman I'll call Rosalind Stein. She was from New york city, where she was some sort of freelance art entrepreneur. She had expanded her operations to Mexico and was an advisor to a archaeological museum.

She had heard about my work and come to check it out.

After a quick glance around, she nodded, and offered me a job at the Museum. "We have l lots of bits and pieces lying around, Broken statuary, arms and heads and whatnot. I'd like to hire you to put some of them together to make complete figures."

I had to keep to a workshop at the back of the Museum. It would not do to have a gringo employee walking around the gallery. I sat or stood at a big sturdy table with hundreds of pieces, most of them at least hundreds of years old, spread in from of me. I had to pick and choose fragments to repair figures or make totally new ones; new old ones.

"These fragments are mostly Olmec, Toltec, Aztec."

"How can I tell the difference. I mean you don't want me to make a woman with an Aztec head and Toltec body."

"Oh, you're a naïve one, aren't you? You don't look it. Don't worry about all that. We'll call the result whatever we want to. If we're short on Toltec, we'll say the piece is Toltec."

"But, Rosalind, that's . . ." I didn't know how to put it.

She finished the sentence for me: "history."

Well, if she didn't care, I didn't. In fact, I started to stretch out, incorporating found objects into the pieces. I sprinkled cigar ash on a figurine; it made for a nice patina.

Rosalind never said a word until I brought in a rusted toilet bowl float.

This museum gig kept us going for a few months until Mary Anne went back to Florida. She missed America and didn't like Mexico although she was half Mexican. I went to Oaxaca for a little while and made contact with Lo Mano Magica Gallery on the main cobblestone street in the beautiful little city. It was run by a Canadian woman and a local native who was a weaver. I showed them photos of my art work, and they were interested.

"Can you bring us three or four pieces in a few days?."

I said I could despite the fact that I had no tools or raw materials or even a place to work. I checked out of my hotel and moved into a small apartment over a bakery. Come daylight I was walking the streets looking for scraps. There was nothing lying around. Everything was used, little was discarded.

But on the roof of the bakery I found stuff and immediately set to work with a few newly purchased tools. The first piece I made was a figure with a pot lid head and a bit of a vacuum cleaner hose for a month truck. I called him the Monster that devoured 'D.F which is a nickname for Mexico City which is in the Distrito Federale'

One day on the zocalo, I saw a chubby gringo with a white strip of sunblock running the length of his nose. He was wearing a Chicago Bulls t-shirt.

I went back to my rooftop and immediately put together a two-foot tall chubby legged figure wearing shorts and a Chicago Bulls t-shirt to which a name plate was pinned announcing that his name was Bob. I painted his face pink and painted a white strip down his nose. His little chubby hand was extended to be shaken.

I took Bob and the Monstre and another small piece to La Mano Magica, a couple of days before I left Oaxaca to return to Canada. Back in Canada and back to landscaping. I was working at Spanish Banks on the west side of town, at a doctor's house overlooking the water. I had worked there every Friday afternoon with Willow and when

Rob and Ellen moved to Tuwanek on the Sunshine Coast I continued to come by. I liked the doctor and his wife, and we always had a drink after I was done for the day.

One afternoon, he pointed to a pile of rubble down the slope. I could see cement chunks, small rocks, broken tile and shards of pottery.

"I want to have three have wide steps leading down the slope, like patio steps, and I'd like to have them with a sort of mosaic surface using that stuff over there. Could you do that for me?"

I told him I thought I could do that although didn't tell I'd never worked with cement except to cart it in a wheelbarrow. But I set to work. I built forms, shovelled in gravel, mixed the cement with sand and water—after looking up information about how much of each to use—and spread it in the form, using a long two by four with a one by four strip nailed across the bottom edge and adjusted according to how much below the form you wanted the surface to reach, You Lay this contraption across the form and pushed and pulled it back and forth creating a level surface' in the case of this first job, about four inches below the top of the form. Into this four-inch sub platform you poured more cement and stuck in the rock, the tile and the pottery shards. I didn't at first realize how much easier the job would be if I were only using one element. Were you just making a tile mosaic you could set the tile on the cement bed and when it had adhered, smooth more cement over it as your grout.

After making these platform steps I got a job assisting a Sicilian stone mason in making a low, mortared stone wall. This required selecting of the stone. The person who's hired you may get nervous about the length of time it has taken for you to get the stone to the site, and then he's liable to be frustrated as he sees you staring at the wall or where the wall is supposed to be. He never understands you're not being lazy just trying to decide what to put where.

I discovered I liked the work and it seemed to come to me naturally. I worked with him on another job, a mosaiced head stone in a cemetery. The cracks in his short thick hands and fingers were permanently caked with cement dust.

Working with him I found myself wishing I had begun learning stone work earlier. I would have made more money to finance my writing and my travel.

I was emboldened to search out stone work on my own. My first independent job was an eight foot-tall cement post in Sechelt at the top of which I installed a bird house.

Soon I was combining the stone and mosaic work with landscaping. In the meantime, I got a regular job at the Rockwood Centre in Sechelt. They had a man who came around to cut the grass so I tended the plants and did the trimming, cutting and pruning.

This job only lasted a few months, I was eager to get back on my own and do more stone work. I lucked into a great job at a place in Gibsons across from the post office. There I installed palm trees, bananas, a New Zealand Fern, pampas grass, yuccas, fucschia and other plants that called to mind those you'd see in tropical climates. As well, I did mosaic work, a walkway, walls, wall pieces and a ten-foot tall mosaiced pillar that held a television set so the owner could sit under her palm trees and watch her favourite shows while neighbours watched her.

As I did this work people would walk by and give me advise. For instance: "You should add more water to your cement mix." Then they'd stand there waiting for you to do it and want to argue if you didn't. Now and again people, usually men but not always, assured me that the palm tree I was planting would never grow. One guy laughed when I put the banana (muso basjoo) in the ground. "You're crazy to think that'll survive" he said, smirking and shaking his head at my stupidity. That house was eventually torn down and the ground bulldozed. I don't know what happened to the banana and most of the palms but the Fern and one of the palms are the ones I mentioned earlier that are flourishing across the road.

Back on the coast I got a rewarding assignment at the house of an acquaintance in the Shaughnessy section of Vancouver.

They had a long and wide back yard but no landscaping had been done. The wife was in favour of a straight cement walk down the middle of the lot, leading from the back door of the house to the laneway. I replied that I thought that might look to rigid. I suggested a curving walkway which would be enhanced by the planting of trees and bushes in the curves. I was surprised when they went along with my idea. The job took a long time to complete but they were pleased with the result and so was I.

One day I got a telephone call from the editor at Canadian Business Magazine with an assignment. Being a guy with a reputation for being a beatnik or alternate culture type who'd written on adventure travel and weird homes and people, I finnd it peculiar that the only editors who'd ever contacted me to write for them have been with business or life style magazines.

"There's a man out your way, in Kelowna who's just been awarded a quarter of a million dollars by the Supreme Court of British Columbia on the grounds that he was prevented from conducting legitimate business and sentenced to prison and to a crazy house. It's all supposedly due to the fact that he owned an island in Lake Okanagan where he planned to develop an Arab theme park. After he served his time, he went back to Beirut and took the Canadian Embassy hostage. "He sounds like your kind of subject. Go check him out and let me know what you think."

I did so. Eddy Haymour lived with his wife Pat and a daughter, Lailah, in a house in the hills in Peachland. He was a dark man with bushy eyebrows and big expressive black eyes. As he outlined his case to me, the injustices he'd suffered, tears came to his eyes.

All he'd wanted to do was develop his theme park on his Rattlesnake Island., but he was thwarted, he claimed, every time he applied for a required permit. In frustration, he began work anyway but was immediately shut down.

Haymour cried injustice and let everyone know he had been cheated and mistreated. His behaviour grew increasingly erratic and he was sentenced to an asylum in New Westminster, B.C. But Haymour told me his actions were solely the result of his unfair treatment.

After the asylum, he did a short stretch in Okalla Penitentiary.

He was released from Okalla, in exchange for handing Rattlesnake Island over to the Provincial government.

"So, I went back to Beirut and rounded up six of my cousins. We got submachines and took over the Embassy. No shots were fired. No one was injured."

His only demand was that his case be heard in the Supreme Court. The presiding judge was Gordon MacKinnon. He was awarded the quarter of a million dollars with which he built an Arabian Nights theme hotel on a hill in Peachland, south of Kelowna.

He told his story with tears in his eyes, and convinced me that he had been grossly mistreated. The article I produced for *Canadian Business Magazine* said as much.

I considered him a sort of hero, one lone man standing up

against the government and all its bylaws and edicts and institutions.

Not long after the article appeared, Haymour showed up at the door of my apartment in Vancouver holding a bushel of apples. He looked at me with sad, happy eyes, bowed his head and handed me the bushel.

We went for coffee and he invited me to come to Peachland and manage his hotel. I was immediately taken with the idea of managing an Arabian Nights Hotel, earning a salary had something to do with it. "Don't make your decision right away. Come out with your girl friend if you have one, and spend a weekend at the Castle. No charge. See what you think."

We went out there and were treated well. Eddy was solicitous and we watched him dealing with guests and diners. He presented his idea to me in detail. His wife Pat said nothing while he was making his pitch but later she took my friend aside and told her, "Whatever Jim is thinking, Eddy is three steps ahead of him."

As we were leaving on Sunday afternoon, she whispered to me, "Think very hard before making up your mind."

I thought about it. I was to live in different rooms in the Castle, depending on which were available. Aw well, Eddy and I would split the price of an automobile which I'd use for hotel business, and I'd get a salary. But the cherry on top was that after a couple of years I'd receive a bonus of a piece of land in the area. I loved the desert-like Okanagan terrain with its mild winters and rolling dun-coloured hills.

Back in the city, I prepared to leave again. When Nicola told me what Pat had said to her, I was irritated. I recalled feeling the same way when during my research for the article I reached his first wife by phone in Alberta.

"I don't want to talk about the lying bastard, I'm afraid."

It took me about an hour at Castle Haymour to realize that its owner was crazy.

He would mutter negative or even violent comments about certain guests. Ones that he believed had done him wrong were particular objects of his wrath, others he just didn't like the look of.

Eddy was vague about my duties. When I asked him what exactly I'd be doing, he replied. "My dreams will be your dreams and you're dreams will be my dreams."

This turned in to me mixing drinks and ordering beer and wine, as well as going around trying to sell ads in the new old Buick I bought.

Soon my dream was that Eddy would get around to paying his half of the car. He did pay my salary the first time. then I was dreaming of getting the next week's. There was always a logical sounding excuse. I'd call all at business to hand out my flyer, and tell about the advantages of promoting the Castle. I rarely had the opportunity to go through the whole spiel. I either got an abrupt, "No thanks," or a harangue about that "Damned terrorist bastard Haymour." I was still naïve enough to ascribe these reactions to them being small-minded provincials, WASPS the bunch of them who had never encountered an Arab before. They still hadn't gotten used to the odd Sikh or Hindu who worked in the local orchards.

Eddy's father was a Moslem and his mother a Christian. He told me, and I heard him tell others, that the name 'Haymour' is featured prominently in the Koran. In reality, it isn't mentioned at all.

When the dining room was occupied, Eddy, in his best Bedouin outfit would sit in a chair ostentatiously fingering his beads. Often when diners who didn't look local, began their meals, he would go their table, sit down uninvited and relate his long tale of woe.

In his brochures he promoted honeymoon suites and romantic getaways, yet it never occurred to him that perhaps people might not wish to be disturbed by his victim stories. On the other hand, maybe he thought he cut a romantic figure and would add a touch of exotica to their Castle Haymour experience.

When I came back to the Castle and reported no sales, he told me I wasn't selling because I looked like a gangster. When I finally revealed that he and his Castle didn't have the finest reputation. he didn't believe me.

When people started sending the beer and white wine back, complaining the beer was flat and the wine off, he blamed it on me. I couldn't figure this out until one night when we were closing up the dining room, he unplugged the fridge. When I asked him why he did this, he looked at me like I was stupid, "To save electricity, of course."

When I tried to explain that you couldn't change the temperature like that without spoiling the product, that only lowered his idea of my intelligence.

He called up a friend, well, an acquaintance; it turned out he had no friends, and asked about the situation. The person told him I was right and that just increased his antipathy.

He arranged a surprise wine tasting for me. One afternoon he suggested we go for a drive but wouldn't tell me where we were going. He drove to a winery up in the hills. There on a long table in the middle of a room were glasses and bottles of wine. I was asked by the owner to taste one wine after another and then rank them by taste and quality. It wasn't difficult to tell the good ones from the bad because most of them were over sweet plonk.

When I put them in order by quality and the wine

Stewart agreed with my choices, Eddy was furious. He fumed all the way back to the Castle and must have put me on his hit list.

On the second day I was in Peachland, Eddy brought up the idea of me writing his life story. I demurred saying I had enough projects on the go. He couldn't understand any story being more worthy than his own.

He kept on and told me he had hired other writers but they weren't up to the task. He still had copies of their manuscripts as well as boxes of personal papers. He invited me to look at them. I did so and immediately ascertained that every version of events was different. He must not have realized that some of his would-be ghost writers had made tape recordings and that these had been transcribed. Versions of incidents differed with each telling. Of course, there was no way to tell which account was the true one.

I didn't really care because I wasn't going to write his book. He was obsessed with his story and reading the transcriptions became oppressive.

Eddy and Pat were not getting along. He said to me, "She's a Canadian woman, I can't hit her. I'm going to go back to Lebanon and get an Arab wife. I can beat her and she won't say anything."

He really did have a hit list. Most of those on the list were petty officials whom he wanted to hurt or humiliate but there were a couple that he insisted demanded serious retribution. At the top of list was former B.C Supreme Court Justice and Provincial Conservative Party Leader, Davey Fulton. The man had refused to hear his case when he was on the bench.

"I want to kill his daughters," Eddy told me one day.

"But Eddy, his daughters didn't do anything to you. Wouldn't it make more sense to kill him?"

He shook his head slowly and looked at me like I was an idiot, beyond comprehension.

"If I kill him," Eddy said, "He won't suffer."

Once he talked about his father and what a great man he was, and provided an example: "I wrote to him one time and told him I was having trouble with someone in Kelowna. And you know what he told me?"

The tears formed in Eddy's eyes, "He said, he'd come to Canada and kill him for me."

On my final day at the Castle, it appeared as if he intended to kill me. I had told him I found it impossible to work for him or even be near him. It was in the afternoon, there were no patrons. It was just He and I, us, Pat and their daughter, Lailah.

When I told him he owed me a couple of months pay, plus half of the money I paid for the car, he was incensed and rushed out of the room. He returned a few minutes later he was wielding a four foot length of two-by-four studded with protruding spikes and thick nails. When he got near me he took a swing.inging. I jumped out of the way and kept moving, circling left, circling right. Between swings he told me what a rotten human being I was.

"And you, Eddy. What a fine memory this is to leave with your daughter."

Pat was horrified, and put her hands over her daughter's eyes. Eventually, he gave up out of exhaustion. Between gasps, he demanded I hand him back the keys to the Castle. There was not a chance that I was going to get that close to the maniac so I threw the keys on the rug. Twenty years later I happened to meet David Mackinnon who is from New Westminster but lives in Europe. His father was Gordon Mackinnon, the Supreme Court Justice who awarded Haymour the quarter of a million dollars. David Who had recently read up on Haymour, just shrugged at his father's decision. "Well, he was working with the information he had at the time."

Back in Vancouver I got a telephone call one afternoon from the head of Yaletown Productions, a film company in the city.

"We'd like to do a documentary series based on your researches into weird homes. We want you to go out looking for these places." And that's how I got to be flying into airports, picking up rental cars and driving around North America from northern B.C. to Georgia Maine to Manitoba. And they paid me to do this.

One Saturday afternoon Collier had been driving in Surrey, B.C. listening to the CBC show Basic Black. He heard me telling the host Arthur Black about the bizarrely personalized homes and gardens I had come across in my wandering.

I'm not talking about geodesic domes, haybale or hobbit houses; No, I mean truly strange, like the beautiful home in the Kootenay Mountains in British Columba that its owner constructed with 50,000 embalming fluid bottles or the place in Houston, Teas draped entirely with aluminum tabs from pop top beer cans.

These homes were the products of the febrile imaginations of men and women who had never for a moment thought of themselves as artists, but they were, of course. These kinds of homes and gardens, some call them 'environments' are vanishing now and not being replaced. Building permits and laws whose sole purpose seems to be to assure homogeneity, mitigate against their creation. Add to this exorbitant real estate prices and the fact that most people these days don't have the manual versatility to build them.

Invariably the homes and gardens were done by working people who knew how to put boards together, to make stone walls albethey unusual ones, to weld, to glue and clamp, to shape and form. But most of all they had unfettered imaginations.

The greatest thing about the job was driving around and accidently finding the sites. I loved the sense of discovery, that kick in the eye that turning the corner revealed.

This lack of method was generally my method in the United States. I found that if I started conversations with people in coffeeshops they tried to avoid me. Should I approach someone on the street, they'd think I meant them harm. This was not the case in Canada, where I could, for instance, join a table of farmers in Saskatchewan on their coffee breaks and simply ask, "Any unusual homes or gardens around here?"

"You want a cinnamon bun with your coffee? There's an old fellow near Elk Horn, lives in a sod house and has a driveway lined with antlers. That the kind of thing you're looking for?"

Pearl Fryar lived in a nice house on a three-acre lot in Bishopville, South Carolina. Every night when he came home from his shift at the factory, he worked on his topiary garden Pearl had seen a picture somewhere and got hooked on the ancient art. He didn't just clip and trim his shrubs into odd shapes, he grafted little branches, the result being incredibly intricate and graceful forms. I learned that his neighbours, all white, resented him despite the fact that he was one of the friendliest men you could meet. It was just that his property was so much nicer than any of theirs.

Volllis Simpson in North Carolina had spent his working life with heavy equipment, designing and building it, repairing and transporting it. He never stopped working with metal, after retiring he just didn't have to put in regular hours. He started constructing whirligigs, welding metal bits into figures, some recognizable, others wildly abstract. These he mounted on towers. The field outside his property became a whirligig farm. His work got a lot of attention and he was besieged by visitors and written up as an artist. He denied it when I visited him, saying "I just make stuff."

And I liked his workshop. It was like a fantasy out of a 1952 *Popular Mechanic's* magazine. He might have built a rocket ship in there, one circa 1890. When I met Vollis Simpson I was immediately reminded of his counterpart who lived diagonally across the continent at a backwater on Vancouver Island. This was George Sawchuk, another big handed working man who could make anything although their was a different political persuasion between he two men. Sawchuk came from Kenora, Ontario where he grew up studying Marxism. He left as soon as he was "tall enough to reach the second rung of a boxcar ladder.".He jumped the freights wherever he thought there might be work. In British Columbia Sawchuk was injured while working on a construction project in the Fraser Valley in1956 A load of steel slipped and crushed His leg. He'd pleaded with the doctors to "buck the Jesus leg off." But they wouldn't do it until 1968. After his leg was amputated it was the first time in twelve years that he was free of constant burning pain.

Sawchuk recovered from the operation at the home of friends in North Vancouver. To pass the time he 'made things' out of wood and put the finished product on fence posts in the yard. Fortune smiled from the other side of the fence. The neighbours were art curators and introduced themselves. "They told me I was an artist and what I was doing had a precedent in art history. I never thought of myself as an artist. Not for one minute. As for art history, I knew nothing about it."

Success may have been uncourted, but it showed up right anyway and right away. Within a couple years of first setting his piec on a fence post, he had reached near celebrity status.

Sawchuck was able to acquire forested land at Fanny Bay and immediately began to use the property as his gallery. A rack of antlers extend from a tree and over time they've come to look like a tree branches. From the antlers hang a soggy old coat. "That's my monument to told Shiplap Sam. His actual name was Sam Shipsaloff but we had some Italians on the crew that couldn't pronounce it and so to them he was Shiplap Sam"

When Shiplap became old and feeble, Sawchuck let him stay in a small trailer in his property for the rest of his days. "When I was a Young man," Sawchuck recalled." I read Jack London and John Steinbeck and later I vowed not to become like them and betray my principles."

Near the monument to Shiplap Sam is a plaque nonouring the well known labour organizer Ginger Goodwin who was shot dead by B.C. Provincial Police in 1918. Sawchuck fashioned a niche in the trunk of a tree inside of which is a glass and inside of that is a coffin and in the coffin a soft point cartridge, similar to the shell that killed Goodwin.

Sawchuck was inspired to do the piece when he came across Goodwin's untended grave in nearby Cumberland, the mining town where Goodwin lived and worked.

Whenever I think Whenever I think of Ginger Goodwin, I'm reminded of another Wobbly and organizer in British Columbia, Arthur 'Slim' Evans.

Evans was born in Toronto at the end of the nineteenth century and apprenticed as a carpenter.

He began to head west at the age of twenty and worked on farms and in mines along the way. He spent time in the coal mines of Drumheller, Alberta where he tried to organize the workers. He joined the UMWA, the United Mine Workers of America, as well as the Communist Party. The UMWA brass didn't like his politics and had him prosecuted for embezzlement. He was convicted and served three years in prison. He came out more radical than when he went in. Evans joined the IWW and in the midst of the Depression organized and led the On to Ottawa Trek of unemployed workers.

When he got to Ottawa he was ushered into Prime Minister's office and gave Bennett an uncompromising piece of his mind.

In his last years, Evans organized metal workers in trail, B.C. and shipyard workers in Vancouver.

Evans died in Vancouver in 1944 after being struck by a car. It has long been maintained his death was no accident.

In 1998, I went to Central America to trace the route of the 1839-1840 Walker Caddy Expedition whose purpose was to bring back accurate information about the Mayan Ceremonial Centre of Palenque. There had been numerous European visitors to the site but it was shrouded in Myth and speculation. John Walker was a petty official in Belize City, a sort of civic busybody. The Home Office in London had determined the trip should be under taken. In those pre-photography days, expeditions
Were accompanied by artists. John Herbert Caddy was an artist and art teacher from the eastern townships of Quebec.

I followed their exact road insofar as I was able. I a hundred and sixty years, the rivers had changed course and the names of places had changed, often several times. I rode buses, traveled by boat and hiked. I was able to get on a 'chicken bus' across the Peten, the first but, I was told, in many years.

Well, the whole trip from Belize City to Palenque was a great adventure that I've written about elsewhere. But on this trip I became aware of two money making practices of which I had not been aware. Somewhere near Lake Chabo, the bus stopped so that a new driver could take over, I used the opportunity to get out and stretch my legs. The driver invited me to come along with him to his village which was a mile or so back in the jungle. He said there would be a place for me to spend the night.

I don't know what I expected but the village was primitive even by Amazon standards. It was like something from A Hollywood movie of the 30s. There were naked young women, too, if not Hedy Lamar as Tondalayo, quite fetching nevertheless.

In he morning I woke to find most of the village at work making palm crosses for palm Sunday. I sat at a table and watched the people applying themselves to their tasks. They split palm fronds down the centre, folded a piece across the vertical fond, made a nice secure fold in the centre and there was a cross. Aware of my sincere interest I was given my own pieces and told what to do. I'm afraid my attempts left much to be desired. The people were too courteous to laugh.

The next evening, I got on the next bus and rode it to the San

Francisco River where I alighted again, thinking Well, I had an adventure last night, maybe I'll have one tonight. And I did.

There was a shack on pilings that extended into the river, I was having a beer and a bowl of some kind of Chili when I got talking to a man a few years older than me who wore a bandana around his head and a fedora over that.

After half an hour, he got up to leave and invited me to come with him to his place in the back country. He had a long piece of silk wound around his waist that covered an unsheathed machete. As we left the place, I asked myself: What the fuck are you doing?

And myself could give back no intelligent answer.

We drove back in his jeep to a falling down corral where my new friend, Asturias, got two horses which we rode further back into the bush. Finally, we got off the horses, tied them and hiked a mile to a big old wooden house.

Snake skins hung from the roof and shimmered when Asturias lit the oil lamp.

I assumed he treated these skins and sold them in Antigua or Guatemala Citty. I was right but the skins only provided him with "moneda" small money).

I got a hint of his main occupation when I entered the house. There were statues and figurines on every available surfaces. They didn't have the clean look of museum pieces or reproductions from boutiques. He smiled at my astonishment. "These pieces must be worth a million dollars."

"At least," he replied. "To the buyer at the other end."

He employed four or five hueccharos to who had contacts with the cutters back in the bush. They would turn over anything they found to the huecharos in exchange for a few cruzieros which they were glad to have. They gave the pieces to Astorias for a few bucks more.

Astorias showed me a two-foot tall stellae that one of his scouts had brought in just that morning. "Four hundred thousand American dollars," he said. "That's what the man in Berlin will pay."

Astorias would be off to Antigua in a couple of days where he'd meet with the first link in the international network. This man an archaeologist would assess the pieces and send a report to Berlin or Paris or Vienna.

Astorias would also be using the internet at a café in the beautiful old city. He kept a small apartment in Guatemala City, maintained a Website and dealt with email. Afterall his was an international business .

During those couple of days with him I couldn't get the totally incongruous thought out of my head from an early 1960s song where a guy is lost in the jungle. And it's in there now as I write this.—"Meanwhile back in the jungle. "

Meanwhile back in the jungle at Astorias' shack I was nearly as surprised to see hundreds of books as I was to see the figurines and sculptures. They were mostly on the history of Guatemala and the surrounding country as well works on exploration and general archaeology. None of them mentioned John Herbert Caddy.

He and Walker reached Palenque months ahead of their America rivals, James Stephens and Frederick Catherwood, but the Americans got the credit of 'discovery.'

Walker wrote a dry report about the journey and Caddy produced a hundred drawings. All of this vanished into the archives of the British foreign office.

Stephens wrote a book about the trip which is still in print and Catherwood's drawings are ubiquitous with both Palenque and Maya archaeology.

Only a few of Caddy's drawings, from his journals, have survived. They are just as interesting and accomplished as the American's.

The next winter, I went to Puerto Escondido, Mexico with a couple of friends, Paul Murphy and Brad Benson both older me, who had begun there on work careers when I was still watching *The Cisco Kid* on television.

Paul was a long time Member of the New Democratic Party, a one-time street kid from Montreal. He and his loquaciousness were utilized by the Party when he was sent out as advance man for NDP candidates. He'd go into a town where the would-be Premier was to speak, secure the venue and generally organize the event. Often these were areas hostile to any notion that might have been thought to be a half-step to the left of centre.

Brad Benson came from a different sort of environment and had a different history of employment. His father had owned a furniture store in Iowa City, Iowa. Brad went to good schools and got with a bank in Chicago when he was done university. "In the late Sixties, I'd ride to work on the Elevated and from my seat I'd sometimes I'd see demonstrations going on outside. I got curious."

He quit his job at the bank and went to British Columbia but his motives had not been political. "I followed a woman."

In Vancouver, he again worked in a bank. All day he approved or rejected loan applications. "I got sick of it and quit", Brad told me. "Then I started a carpet business. When that didn't amount to much, I was thoroughly fed up and became a carpenter's apprentice."

He discovered he had an innate talent for his new trade and was able to operate a successful business on the Sunshine Coast.

The three of us rented a large ground floor apartment with a courtyard in Puerto Escondido. The building was owned by a Greek man who used to run a construction company in Toronto. It turned out I had done landscape work on a couple of properties he had built. When he asked me if I was still in that line of work, I replied that now I was concentrating on yard sculptures. The result of this confab was a eight foot tall zig zag sculpture that is still standing at the front of the building. Brad made the form and helped me pour cement. I mosaiced it with tile that the owner purchased. Mexicans don't throw away much.

We all had a good time in Mexico with trips to Guatemala and up into the mountains but finally it was time to return to Canada. Brad drove back to B.C. with one of my larger wooden figures next to him in the passenger's seat and strapped in with a seat belt. "This way," he said I can use the HOV lanes in the States."

Murphy and I flew back arriving in late March on a gray drizzly day exactly like the day we got on the plane back in November.

I started landscaping again but after a few months made up my mind to move back East. I was not quite sixty and felt in good shape. I had two solo art shows scheduled in Toronto and figured they might be able to generate some momentum.

I arrived in Toronto in the midst of the hottest summer on record. It was thirty degrees C. for several days in a row and three days the temperature rose to over forty. It was no time to look for landscaping work. I did stop into a variety shote that had a help wanted sign in the window. It was for a construction job. The Korean man behind the counter laughed at me, "You too old. Too old. Hah, hah."

I celebrated my sixtieth birthday tearing out the innards of a house far up Avenue Road. It was tough work carting beams and drywall down the stairs and into the front yard. When the debris was gone, painting began. This job lasted a couple of weeks then I stumbled into another one. I came across a notice for a correspondence college called Granton Institute. The Institute had been around for decades and offered courses on a hundred different subjects. The students dealt via mail with an expert in their chosen field. I was hired as the expert in Landscaping, Journalism and Anatomy and Physiology.

I worked in a big room with twenty other 'experts.'

It felt strange at first working inside but I got used to it, and there never was any dissension with my fellow workers. The work wasn't difficult and I could come and go as I pleased. I particularly liked the trip to work in the morning and the return at night. When the weather permitted, I walked to work. It was about a mile and half and thanks to the Toronto parks system—which assured there was a block square park every couple of streets, I was able to cover most of the distance on grass. After a month at Granton I was given a promotion. I found my job title to be the height of irony. I was made the Career Counselor. I did this and the other work as a tutor.

People would call or write from all over Canada to ask me whether they should pursue a career in computers or maybe auto mechanics. On the one hand, I certainly didn't consider myself qualified to give advice; on the other hand, who is?

After a couple of months, the irony began to seem like hypocrisy and I resigned.

With no job and a few bucks in my pocket I did what I usually did in such circumstances I went on a trip. This one was to Vietnam with Brad Benson. We travelled throughout the country. I had no way of knowing it was the first of many trips to Vietnam.

The next year I was back with another friend and we rented a house for seven months. We were the only Westerners on the street or in the entire District for all I could tell. My friend got on as a teacher of English, while I spent most of my time pursuing the noble calling of flaneur or making glass sculptures on our roof. I managed to place a couple of these in a Vietnamese gallery but the owner, told me, "Our tastes are much too conservative for your kind of work. You could probably sell some in Phenom Penh."

One day I came across a little story in the *Vietnam News* about rampaging elephants killing several people in the Central Highlands. The article suggested the herd was incensed by human encroachment on its territory. I was astounded, first to realize that Vietnam had wild elephants—I thought they only existed in Africa and India—and second by the fact that the attacks were a group effort. Most elephant attacks are the work of rogues cut off from their herd and driven mad by pain or loneliness. There seem to be very few recorded incidents where the animals conspired to kill humans.

In the newspaper's archives I discovered reports of other deadly attacks, in several provinces going back over a number of years, but mostly in the Central Highlands near the Laotian and Cambodian borders. The stories had a common theme: jungles are the natural habitat of elephants; as the jungles are depleted the animals have less space to forage and reproduce, they become enraged and strike back.

At first the attacks had occurred when the elephants came upon a human in the course of their wandering. Most recently, though, it seemed as though the animals had gone looking. The government tried all sorts of schemes, such as relocating them or bringing Malaysian mahouts -experienced elephant handlers—to consult. Nothing worked.
The rogue herd had already been moved to the country's largest national park, Yok Don, in Dak Lak province, but no sooner had they snapped

out of their tranquilized stupor than they went on a foray beyond the park, trampling anyone they came upon and making for the village of Ban Don, where they destroyed several houses before returning to the jungle. It seemed very much like a warning.

That's what intrigued me: the elephants were clearly thinking and planning. I am aware that we love to anthropomorphize these great beasts, writing cutesy-poo songs about the way the babies walk. Rendering them cuddly in cartoons, claiming to see pink ones when drunk. But I could find no explanation for what they had done here, for their method. They had a purpose and were communicating with each other.

What animals kill you and walk away? We fear man-eating lions and tigers, jaguars and crocodiles but if one of them kills you it is probably because they want to eat you. The bear might have a plan but the biggest grizzly is a tenth of the weight of an Asian elephant. And it doesn't come looking.

I wanted to go to Yok Don Park to see these elephants for myself. I hoped to eventually produce an article about my experiences on the elephant trail but I never considered that I was doing the ground work for another job, one that I would take on but one for which I'd never get paid.

I flew from Saigon to the beach town of Nah Trang then caught a small bus to Buon Ma Thhuot, the largest city in the Central Highlands.

I sat in the back of one ton rice bags, the only Westerner on board. For five hours the bus climbed serpentine roads from the coast, through green hills covered with banana plants and into the high country where the plateaus looked as they they'd been covered with a camel-hair coat. The next day, I rode the remaining fifty-five kilometres to the village of Ban Don on the back of a motorbike.

The people in Ban Don belong to the Ede and Mnong tribes. There are no more than twenty houses in the village and most of the men are elephant handlers, their main work, when I was there being the domestication of the wild animals that haven't been relocated in the park—at least the one that were deemed tameable. Walking around the village and could hardly help bumping, literally, into elephants that, just months before, had roamed free. I saw Vietnamese tourists climbing up on a work elephant to have their photos taken.

The ranger in charge of the other killer elephants was a tall, lean and fierce-looking man who spat when I mentioned the tourists. When I asked that he lead me to the wild elephants, he told me, through the translator, that he thought I was a crazy old guy, but he eventually agreed.

But the next day the ranger begged off, claiming he had to stay in bed to nurse a cold, so I set out for the jungle on my own. Two fishermen took me across the Ea Krong river in a dugout canoe, and then I started walking. My directions were cursory: follow the trail until it narrows and branches off; then keep to the one on the right.

The farther I walked, the denser the jungle became, but despite the presence of wildlife, there was not the humid, insect-laden oppressiveness of the Amazon or the jungles of Panama. The trees were not as tall, the understory not as dense. I could see the sky at all times, blue as a baby's blanket.

About eight kilometres in I came across a clearing where the ranger had set up a tent and stored his gear. He'd fashioned an enclosure of bamboo stakes plaited with hardwood saplings. Beyond the enclosure, several metres away, stood a young elephant, a male about two-and-a-half metres tall at the head.

A thick iron cuff encompassed one ankle, and a chain linked the cuff to an auger in the ground. Its eyes were slivers of orbs. When I moved to my right, the animal's left eye moved to follow me. Otherwise, it was motionless, taking me in. I thought of the eyes of the tamed animals back in the village. Eyes that were unclear, as if covered by some veil of defeat. I thought of the beasts at the Saigon Zoo, swaying their trunks back and forth in despair, back and forth. I stepped away from the enclosure and was turning when the animal let out a bellow that seemed to shake the trees.

After walking another four kilometres, I came to a second clearing and was about to start back when I saw a full-grown elephant about a quarter of a mile away in a patch of second-growth forest that had probably been defoliated by the Americans during the war. They also bombed elephants from B-52s with the excuse that every elephant was a potential transporter of goods for the Viet Cong along he Ho Chi Minh Trail.

The elephant had to be one of killers otherwise it wouldn't be there. I stood still, watching him, remembering what a mahout in the village had told me:

"We don't want to share our terrain with that which we fear, with something other than ourselves that can 'think' and is dangerous."

I watched the elephant until the picture of him the way he is supposed to be, was burned into my brain to stay.

After my experience with elephants and the game farm, I wrote another article for *Walrus Magazine* about land mines in Cambodia where I had gone out in the field with mine-clearing crews.

I spent considerable time in Phnom Penh, the capitol which is situated on the Mekong River known in Cambodia as the Tonle Sap.

A couple of months after the article appeared I was contacted by a woman in Texas who wished to do her Doctoral thesis on Cambodia and the Pol Pot regime. She wanted information from soldiers who had done the bidding of that maniac who eliminated half the population of that country. Like Hitler he had written and broadcast his plans.

The woman wanted to know if I'd be of assistance so I got in touch with her. I told her straight off that there was a village near the Laos border where these men had fled and were not bothered. Elsewhere in the country they'd be murdered.

She hired me to go and get information from these men. To tape them when if it was possible and to take photographs when possible. I agreed to allow her to claim the research and adventure as her own. I was paid me handsomely for the privilege.

I was assisted in this endeavour by a couple of Cambodian Army men I befriended when I went out on the mine clearing expedition. From them I got logistical advice and names of people near the village who might be helpful.

So I made the trip. When I alighted from the plane in Phnom Penh, I heard my name called. It was a driver named Remy who I had once hired to take me around the city and with whom I had become friends.

Remy had advice but regretted he couldn't come with me and wreck some havoc. "Plenty of guards and guns there."

He was right. I can't reveal much about this adventure because of the deal I made with the woman.

No sooner was I back in Toronto than I got another foreign assignment about which I can't go into detail either.

This was the outcome of a Columbian tango instructor of all things. I had met her in a city in New Zealand where she ran a studio. She had grown up in Buenos Aires and spent her youth and early girlhood studying tango. In her twenties she married a Columbian and moved with him to Medellin. After the breakup she followed another guy to New Zealand. She told a Colombian journalist in exile in Toronto about me and the result was that a couple of months after returning from Cambodia, I was in Bogota at the same hotel I had stayed at thirty years earlier when doing a story about the burgeoning new cocaine business.

All I had to do was deliver a message to a woman in a coffee shop of the Hotel Tequedama. I was supposed to look like I didn't have a clue about anything and it was suggested that I dress like a typical American tourist but there I drew the line. I figured the powers that be, the official ones, would simply take me for some coke mule or low-level dealer and leave me alone.

The message, which I didn't read despite my curiosity—it's best not to transgress in Bogota—had to do with a kidnapping in the mountains. One that made the news not long after I got back to Toronto.

Soon after arriving, I met an Ethiopian man who had just bought an art gallery in the Junction area and asked me to help run the place. He knew nothing about running art galleries but, then, neither did I. Somewhere along the line he had encountered artists. None of them were accomplished in a conservative, old fashioned sort of way. I hung my own stuff on the walls. One of the painters was a short wide Bulgarian man with curly gray hair that covered much of his forehead. He specialized in large oils of peasants working in fields. He had several Bulgarian friends who'd come and visit him at the gallery where he had taken to holding court. One day I noticed him in conversation with another man and they both kept looking over at me.

Finally, the friend came over and said he had a proposition for me.

"I don't like to be propositioned while it's still daylight."
"What?"
"Never mind. What's up?"

He told me had made films for the Eastern European market. Crime films. And would I like to be in some of them. I replied that I would indeed but I didn't speak Bulgarian, Romanian or any other eastern European language. He said that didn't matter, and laid out the deal. I'd wear certain clothes that he'd provide and he'd shoot me in different scenes. I'd talk to other actors. Like the Vietnamese television commercial I could say whatever ever I wished to because it would be dubbed in the language of whatever country the movie was to be released. In other words, my scenes might be shown in four countries with my character speaking four different languages. Most of the scenes were played out along the waterfront. There were cars and guns involved. In all I must have filmed six hours which turned out were used in thirty films. The work was well paid, fun and it was certainly different. Those were nice days, moving around on green grass on fine September days under blue skies. I was disappointed the job only lasted six or seven weeks.

Shortly after, I moved back to the Sunshine Coast and married Cher Monroe whom I met when she worked on the ferry that went between the Sunshine Coast and West Vancouver. She had been a deckhand, traffic director, ramp operator and kitchen worker. she's had nearly as many jobs as I've had, starting age sixteen with Dial-A-Bottle, a legitimate business that was listed in the phone book. In other provinces, Ontario, for instance, it would have been a bootleg operation.

You dialed the number. Cher answered and relayed your request to the dispatcher who sent a driver to your address. She admits that at the time she knew nothing about liquor. First day on the job, she relayed an order for what she thought was Bacardi Rye.

"There was a woman who phoned every morning and asked for between two and five bottles of booze, no mickeys, either."

Cher later worked in a dress hop, a candy store, a supermarket, as a proof reader for a lawyer and obtained her private investigator's license. That fact and my own recent assignments in Cambodia and Colombia convinced me that we should start our own outfit and thus was born Extreme Research. We let it be known that we would take on assignments that went beyond the ordinary. It was not and probably still isn't legal to advertise as a private investigator unless you were licensed. Cher's license had long expired and although I had done work in Toronto and San Francisco, I didn't have a license.

What made it doubly hard to advertise is that discretion is a big part of investigation, and citing references violates the agreement.

I wrote four mystery novels set in Vancouver between 1937 and 1945. In one of them I gave my private eye, Gene Castle a case I had worked. I was being considered for a job at an agency and they gave me a problem to solve. They had a new client who every Thursday received an obituary notice in the mail that had been clipped from a newspaper. There was never a note or any other material in the envelope. So, who did it?

That was an easy one.

First, I realized the obituaries were not from one of the three major dailies. The type face was different. Second, I saw that each was the obituary of a person with a name I took to be Jewish.

At a downtown newsstand, I went through the weekly papers.

The type on the obituaries matched those of the English language Jewish weekly which was published on Wednesdays. In those days the postmark was a circle. Every circle had a short line or a nub extending inward. The position of the nub indicated the station where they had been franked. All my envelopes had been mailed at the Dovercourt post office. I went there and asked one of the clerks if there was anyone who came to the station on Wednesdays, in the afternoon, and posted letters (taking the chance that he was an older fellow and thus took more time to do his errands, and didn't care to put his mail in the box outside).

The man lived a block or two away and had been coming to the Dovercourt post office for years.

"Is he a Jewish guy?"

"Yes, he is."

The clerk told me the man's name and I relayed it do the man at the agency and who in turn gave it to the client. The culprit was a former business partner with whom he had a long-standing feud.

I got the job it didn't last long. There was no trench coat stuff and I didn't pack a heater. Much of the work was industrial spying, but not the high tech stuff that came later where you could sit in your car in the parking lot of an office building and listen to a conversation on the twelfth floor.

No, this was the sneaky kind of thing where you got sent to a warehouse as a worker and reported to management about who was stealing stuff. Either that or they wanted me to prowl around stores and check out whether the produce manager was slipping sacks of carrots to his partner out back. I declined to do this kind of work.

Those foreign investigative jobs came to me unbidden but when we tried to find work for Extreme Research, Cher and I were unsuccessful. It became sort of an in house joke. If something was lost, one of us would say, "This looks like a job for Extreme Research'"

I'm still available.

Twice I went to New Zealand to read poetry in public and I got paid for doing it so that qualifies as work. Both times I went on a 'tour', twelve or fifteen appearances in cities and towns throughout both islands. I've also read in Melbourne, Paris, Berlin and Amsterdam. I rarely get invited to read in Canada, and when I do the organizers usually ask me to do it for free. Some of them can tap the Canada Council for a reading fee. But to qualify for the $125, the prospective reader has to be on the approved poets list. To be on that list you have to be a good little boy or girl. No outliers are permitted.

I was once invited to read and speak to a writing class at Douglas College in New Westminster, B.C. The instructor, Mary Burns wo lives in Gibsons, B.C. said she'd get me the $125 from the Canada Council. I replied that she would be turned down when she submitted my name. Mary told me I was being paranoid and she'd never had a reader rejected. I was rejected.

In Canada, to succeed a writer has to be part of the conservative establishment or part of the avant garde establishment. Independence is not allowed. This isn't sour grapes on my part, it's the depressing truth. In other countries readings provide a writer with a supplement to his or her income or in some countries a decent income.

In New Zealand I've done readings with musicians in clubs where they've had a cover charge. I remember the first time this happened. It was at a club in Dunedin and I wasn't expecting it; in fact, I was intimidated when I saw the sign in the window Ten Dollar Cover. "No one's going to show up," I thought.

But the place was packed and enough money came in that I distributed evenly between the four members of the combo, myself and the sound man, and we each came away with over five hundred dollars. To Canadian ears this probably sounds like an outrageous lie.

Canadians expect culture to be free; other countries are more sophisticated and thus have a healthier cultural life.

Richard Olafson who published several of my books at Ekstasis Editions which he runs in Victoria with his wife Carol Sokoloff got me some paying gigs at three writers' festivals in B.C., all of them on Vancouver Island. The only other Canadian festival I have ever been invited to was in Winnipeg and that was thirty years ago. I haven't been invited to a festival since.

After a show in Christchurch a man came up to me and said, "I guess you make a living at this."

He was one of their leading poets and did make a living from readings. I regretted having to tell him that was not the case with me. I did an afternoon reading at a university in Palmerston North. The money was such that I tried to give half of it back. They wouldn't take it so I sprang for dinner.

I had an interesting time getting to Palmerston North.

The customs official at the airport asked me where I was going and I told him. He told me back that "There is no such place called Palmerston North, and refused me entry. I asked to speak to his superior. This man shook his head and apologized.

After the reading a reporter asked me how my latest New Zealand trip was transpiring and I told him the story. The next day's local newspaper carried the head:
Palmerston North Doesn't Exist! Says Customs official.

I can't remember exactly when I met Freddy Fuller although I'd heard about him in boxing circles. A couple of people told me I should get in touch with him. He had been a successful amateur boxer in British Columbia but as amateur boxing was of little interest for me, I didn't follow up on the suggestions.

Hanging around the gyms and fight clubs, I studied guys hitting the heavy bag and noticed that most pounded away with no pretense of defense. The bag was great for working on your left hook or right hand body shots but you had to stand and slug differently when someone Was trying to hit you back.

It dawned on me then that what was needed was a punching bag that punched back. I started planning and sketching this in whatever spare time I had from my other money-making ventures. The bag had to be substantial enough to withstand constant pounding and it required a frame and a motor. I realized the motor would have to have a governor and I needed some way to vary the motion of the arm-like pads that 'punched' back, otherwise the punches would be predictable and thus easily countered.

I needed a workshop which I didn't have. I wasn't able to figure out the intricacies of the motor; hell, I needed the motor. The frame would have to have thick padding. I would have to hire help to make my punching bag that punches back but I had neither the money to obtains part nor the money to hire someone.

I located a potential investor, a man who worked for a venture capital company who happened to be a boxing fan. He liked my idea and said the cost of making the model would not be prohibitive for him but the real cost would come with the patent search and the need to meet production standards.

If you could get all that done you had to market your baby. How many inventors have a clue about such things?

It must have been this fellow who put me in touch with Freddy Fuller who was a short, stocky energetic man with a thousand ideas. He had devised a paint tray liner made from filmy plastic that could be peeled from the tray when the painting was done. This made the cleanup process more efficient, insured paint wouldn't splatter and you weren't left with dried paint on the tray.

Another thing Freddy devised was a self-watering plant system that allowed your plants to be watered when you were away. You could set it for ten o'clock every morning for three days or three o'clock every Thursday afternoon for a month.

It was either Freddy or the main businessman who got the idea of hiring me to be the liaison between inventors and businessmen. It had been discovered that these two groups could not relate to each other. The businessmen had never dealt with anyone like the usually barmy inventors and the inventors were out of their depth with the money men.

And that's where I came in. I met with the inventors, and some of them, quite frankly, might have been living in another dimension, after which I went to the office and made my report.

The first 'inventor' I spoke with wasn't really an inventor at all. She had a gimmicky item that she wanted marketed. She showed me a cluster of small brown plastic sticks on a plastic base. When I looked puzzled, she smirked. "What's British Columbia most known for?". Before I could answer she said, "Trees, right?"

"Un huh."

"Well these are trees and they represent British Columbia. They'll be very popular. You can make brooches of them. Earrings or fridge magnets."

"But really, they don't look like trees so much as tree stumps. At least that's the polite interpretation."

" "Are you, some kind of tree hugger?"

"No, but a good portion of your potential market is. And that's the polite version."

"You're deliberately being negative. What's the other version?"

"Pardon we for saying it but that cluster of threes or stumps really look like a pile of turds."

She let me have it then. We were on Georgia Street in Vancouver, out front of the White Castle restaurant. A few people walking by looked at us probably wondering that I had done to cause the respectable looking woman to be chastising me.

"Pervert!" she shouted. "You're nothing but a pervert."

"Look, lady. I bet if you were to ask any of these people they'd all you the same thing. It looks like shit."

More hollering after which I took the object and approached the first passerby, a tall young, pale complexioned guy man with dyed black hair and showed him the object, "Excuse me, but would you tell me what this looks like to you?"

He glanced at it and without missing a beat or breaking stride, said, "Looks like a bunch of turds."

Well, this made the woman even angrier, she grabbed the thing from my hand and stomped away but not before saying she as going to report me.

And she did, too but Howard merely laughed.

The next man, the one with the alcohol balls was pleasant and interesting, too.

He lived in a basement apartment on Broadway, just west of main, half the space devoted to his laboratory.

His laboratory consisted of a cafeteria table, cluttered with vials and bottles, a one-burner hot plate and a Bunsen burner. It looked like it had pilfered from an old-time movie where the mad scientist did his absent-minded work.

The balls resembled small jaw breakers. There were gin balls and rye balls, whiskey balls and vodka balls.

You put club soda in a glass, drop in the ball of your choice and before you know it, you Have your vodka and soda, your rye and soda."

"It actually works?"

"You be the judge."

"I'll have a rum and soda."

He dropped a rum ball into some soda and stirred the mixture once the ball had dissolved. He handed it to me.

"Well, what does it taste like?"

"It tastes like a rum and soda."

It did too. The light bulb went on, me thinking this was worth millions.

I could have stayed all day talking to him and doing my research.

Then there was the fellow who had a rocket ship all ready to take off for the moon. He lived in South Burnaby where we met at a Tim Horton's. He was a heavy set man with a walleye. He told about his space ship while gobbling Tim Bits. I must have passed whatever criteria he had in his mind because he invited me back to his place. Instead of the workshop complex I expected to find, we went to his small one storey single house. There were sheets of typing paper with diagrams and formulae scotch taped to the fridge and the walls and the backs of chairs. After assuring me he had done all necessary work and the craft was ready to fly, I asked him how exactly he expected Inventex to assist him.

"I need to get it transported to Langley Air Field where I'll launch it."

"You're going to the moon from Langley Air Field?"

"Sure, I just need permissions, and help preparing for Lift off."

And where can I see your rocket ship?"

"Oh, it's out back."

"You mean out back of your house?"

"Sure thing."

He led me out back, across his yard toward a small garage where I expected to see his invention. I looked through a dirty window but didn't see anything except sheets of tin, piles of scrap lumber, and rolls of carpet.

"No, no. Go out to the lane."

He jerked his thumb at something lying in the weeds between the side of the garage of the surface of the laneway. It was eight or ten feet long, two and a half feet wide and resembled nothing so much as a elongated tin cigar tube. It was rusting away.

"You're telling me that's your space craft?

He beamed like he was displaying his happy little grandson.

"You sure this thing works?"

"Of course."

"Who's going to be your pilot?"

"I am."

There is no way in the world he was going to fit inside the thing, not even if he lost a hundred pounds and lay flat on his back. It was even too small for Olive Oyl.

"Well, what do you think?"

I thought perhaps it was a huge joke but no he was serious. As serious as he was delusional. He was a nice gentle man but seriously crazy. There was no sign of a power train.

"Well," I said. "I don't make the decisions. All I can do is go back to the office and file my report. We'll let you know."

"Oh, thanks so much for coming out and treating me with respect."

I did go back and file a report along with photos of him and his craft. The money men laughed and I became furious at their condescension. I didn't last much longer in that position.

I never did much farm work apart from haying a couple of times, cleaning stables and two weeks on a farm in Saskatchewan, sleeping on a cot in the barn and doing odd jobs around the place during the day. I'm reminded of this after receiving letters recently from Ian Cutler who grew up on the family holding in Wales, and Warren Fraser, raised on a farm in Cookshire, Quebec. Both these men are the same age and were doing the same chores at the same time when they were younger. Warren remembers starting his chores at five in the morning, milking cows and shoveling manure before going to school. There was no time to spare in order to clean up. He was embarrassed to appear at school, smelling like manure. It certainly didn't help him to get a date. After school it was more of the same.

Meanwhile on the other side of the Pond, Ian Cutler was doing the same sort of thing only the animals were pigs rather than cows. He shifted manure and harvested lettuce and strawberries from 5AM until school time.

After school and week ends it was milling corn, watering the animals and creosoting buildings. But Ian attended agricultural college and upon graduating, obtained papers that enabled him to get on as an agricultural research assistant in Northern Zambia. Thus began a career of almost unparalleled diversity, both occupational and in regards human experience. During his years in Africa, Cutler spent his free time travelling through the fields and hills where he encountered all sorts of people. Eventually he returned to Britain and got a job as a street sweeper outside of London. Then he was a mental health nurse and later a general health nurse. He went to Honduras to work as a nurse. Wherever he went he explored the territory. Back in Britain after years away, Cutler eventually became involved in local government.

Warren Fraser went to Toronto and worked on the assembly line of a telephone company. After a couple of years of that he returned to help out on the family farm.

He remembers how in the early spring the winter manure in the cow yards was often a foot deep and very mucky. One afternoon while trying to separate a cow from the herd, one of his his rubber boots was sucked off 'by the gooey, deep sludge'. So, there he was wading through the muck with one stockinged foot and one rubber boot.

He managed to free himself and get out of there but a day or two later was back in the barn and the muck, "I hollered at a heifer and "my top denture went flying into the smelly dung."

He was soon back in Toronto.

John Montgomery was a character in a few of Jack Kerouac's novel. He was Morley Coughlin who climbed the Sierra Nevada Matterhorn in *Dharma Bums*, and Alex Fairbrother in *Desolation Angels*, "the crazy satirist of the whole scene." One day Kerouac received a box of girl scout cookies in the mail from Montgomery.

In that book Montgomery hires Kerouac to shovel out the basement of a house he'd bought in Mill Valley. Meanwhile, Montgomery was working on laying down a patio. He'd buy houses, fix them up and sell them.

One day after I'd met Montgomery by mail, the post man brought me a large box of cookies, t-shirts and socks. There was also a discarded library book, from Nevada all about America's concentration camps.

Montgomery hired me to make a parking pad outside another house in Mill Valley. I'd be shovelling gravel or spreading cement and Montgomery would come rushing out of the house, grab whatever tool I was using, make a few frantic motions, saying, "You have to move fast like this."

The he'd hand me back the shovel or rake and head back into the house to write a crazy poem or study his Farsi lesson, while I continued working for another five hours.

Kerouac was so frustrated by his experience with John, he wrote, I promised myself I'd never do another day's 'work' at a job…ever again come hell or high water.'

When I was done working for John, I was so frustrated I made myself the same promise. Kerouac, at least, kept his promise.

Born in Richmond, Virginia on July 14, 1945, Jim Christy grew up in South Philadelphia, a tough area featured in his autobiographical novel *Streethearts*, and also featured in Sylvester Stallone's *Rocky* movies. "Boxing was in the air," he once recalled. "You knew people who had boxed; if Dickens had been around he would have written about boxing." Christy later wrote about boxing as a business and a sub-culture, in *Flesh & Blood*. Christy began running away from home around age 12, once getting as far as the outskirts of Buffalo. He befriended one of his closest friends and mentors, Floyd Wallace, a hobo, a former boxer and a former soldier of fortune, and learned to ride the freights at a young age. Christy came to Canada in October of 1968, to evade the Viet Nam war draft, and was active in co-founding two shortlived underground press publications in Toronto. His first book concerned draft resisters in Canada. Christy became a Canadian citizen as soon as possible. While researching *Rough Road to the North*, he became fascinated by the life of Charles Eugene Bedaux, and subsequently wrote a biography called *The Price of Power*. Other outsiders who have struck Christy as heroes include a veteran carnival performer named Marcel Horne, jazz musician Charlie Leeds, leftist Emma Goldman and explorer Sir Richard Francis Burton.

Jim Christy first came to Vancouver in December of 1981 to promote his novel *Streethearts*, and he has remained on the West Coast, adopting Gibsons on the Sunshine Coast as his home base. An artist, gardener, prolific freelance journalist and an ex-regular on American Bandstand, Christy has evolved his own "King of the Road" outsiderism into a cool-headed series of "noir" fiction featuring a tough-talking private detective in Vancouver named Gene Castle. The series opens in 1937 with *Shanghai Alley* and moves forward to 1939 in the second Gene Castle gumshoe mystery, *Princess and Gore*, a title drawn from two street names in Vancouver's Downtown Eastside. The third Castle mystery is *Terminal Avenue*, another title drawn from a street name. It features the bullet-eating detective searching for the kidnapped daughter of a Nazi resistance leader. The series culminated with *Nine O'Clock Gun*.

As a departure from his detective novel series, Christy published *The Redemption of Anna Dupree*, an unconventional love story and a "road novel" about an acid-tongued, elderly actress in her seventies who escapes to Mexico with Colin, a much younger employee of the Okanagan nursing home in which she lives. The protagonist, who formerly appeared in some British and American noir films in minor roles, has been described by reviewer John Moore as an unrepentant bad girl who is "guilty of no crime but her age in a culture that worships youth."

Christy has had his passport stamped in Central America, Greenland, Cambodia, Europe and Brazil. The locales for Christy's non-fiction collection entitled *Between the Meridians* include an annual convention of hobos in Britt, Iowa and the Honduran jungle where he searches for a Golden Madonna, plus memories set in Bogota, Soweto,

Chiapas, Honduras, Rhodesia, New Zealand and Vienna. Other reminiscences introduce a local hit man, a stripper, a lesbian Mom, an aging Russian Count, two homosexual Indian brothers from the Yukon, named Byron and Shelley, and a lovelorn American tourist waiting 20 years for a Mexican gigolo.

Some hype is too good to overlook. According to Guernica Editions, "The poetry in *Marimba Forever* is concerned with love and longing, which the author displays in all their multifarious guises. Many of the poems can be regarded as small films: nourish, action, farce or slapstick; others call music to mind: a tenor saxophone improvising on a standard melody in the wee small hours just as the milk man is getting up and rubbing sleep from his eyes; a roadhouse honky-tonk hell-raiser; six gypsies with accordions and tubas on the back of a flatbed truck somewhere near Ploestki or a marimba orchestra in a tropical town square playing like they never want to stop while palm trees sway and lovers neck on the green benches."

In quick succession, Jim Christy published his 32nd book since 1972, *The Big Thirst and other Doggone Poems* (Ekstasis $23.95), followed by his 33rd, *Rogues, Rascals, and Scalawags Too: Ne'er-Do-Wells Through the Ages* (Anvil $20). Always in search of original characters and experiences, Jim Christy is a literary vagabond who has a follow-up volume to *Scalawags: Rogues, Roustabouts, Wags & Scamps*. The characters profiled for *Ne'er-Do-Wells* include Carolina Otero, Andre Malraux, Lord Timothy Dexter, Suzanne Valadon, William Hunt, Mata Hari, Emma Hamilton, Bata Kindai Amgoza.

www.ingramcontent.com/pod-product-compliance
Lightning Source LLC
Chambersburg PA
CBHW042046280426
43661CB00114B/1458/J